Praise For

Private Equity Investing in Direct Selling

"The power of the direct selling model often is misunderstood by investors and advisors. This book thoughtfully and crisply lays out how and why investing in direct selling can be quite compelling when done correctly."

Eric Roth, Managing Director, Midocean Partners

"Investing in a direct selling business without reading this book is like trying to climb Everest without a Sherpa. No one should invest so much as a dollar in a direct sales business without reading it. Brett Blake exposes this mysterious industry to clear-headed analysis that allows for better diligence and higher investment returns."

Devin Thorpe, Best-Selling Author

"Direct selling is the most misunderstood industry in the world today. Author Brett Blake does a masterful job explaining in easy-to-understand language, what direct selling is—and more importantly, what it's not. Although this book is aimed at the financial community, I see it being a go-to resource within our own industry, the media, as well as anyone looking to understand the channel's unique nuances."

Todd Eliason, Publisher & Editor in Chief, Direct Selling News

"As someone who has followed publicly traded direct sellers since Amway took its Asia-Pacific arm public in 1993, I found that *Private Equity Investing in Direct Selling* is a perfect vehicle for anyone interested in investing in a direct selling company, whether private or public. I found Brett's insights from being both a participant in and an observer of the channel over the years to be invaluable."

Douglas M. Lane, CFA, Principal, Director of Research,

Lane Research

"The success of a crowd-sourced independent salesforce not only requires a relevant and valuable product proposition, but also a respect for the motivational psychology, behavioral economics and game dynamics associated with the direct selling business model. *Private Equity Investing in Direct Sales* provides an insightful and entertaining perspective for newcomers with a view of the many less-than-obvious nuances of operating a business in the direct selling channel."

Lori Bush, Former CEO, Rodan + Fields, and Chair, New Avon

Private Equity Investing in Direct Selling:
Identifying Risk and Rewards

Brett A. Blake

Private Equity Investing in Direct Selling:
Identifying Risk and Rewards

© 2019 Brett A. Blake. All rights reserved.

For more information about this book, to order books in bulk, or to schedule the author for a speaking or consulting engagement contact Brett Blake:

Email: Bblake@investingindirectselling.com
For PDF downloads of handouts mentioned visit:
www.investingindirectselling.com

Library of Congress Control Number: 2019910400

Print ISBN: 978-1-7333568-0-0

eBook ISBN: 978-1-7333568-1-7

Printed in the United States of America.

Cover Design by Madison Noelle Blake

Contents

Acknowledgements

I dedicate this first book to my first love, my first teacher, and my first and most enduring fan, my mother Suzanne Hargreaves Blake, who passed away while I was writing this book on Valentine's Day 2019, after a six-year battle with cancer. While my faith in the resurrection is sure, I still miss her deeply. My mom taught pre-school during my early years and I was her student before and after class. She organized reading contests for my siblings and me in the summer, helped me with my first business— a backyard fair before I was six—and secured my first job as a paper boy at age eight. Mom and dad (Leon)raised one amazing daughter, my oldest sister Darcy, followed by six boys. Our brother Todd was killed in a car accident after just three years on Earth. The other five boys have all tried to make our mom proud.

God be thanked for my angel mother.

I'm grateful for the more twenty-nine CEOs, presidents, investment bankers, private equity professionals, and consultants who allowed me to interview them for this book. Direct selling is unique in the warm relationships executives have with one another and I have been blessed with many, many close friends.

I would not have worked in direct selling were it not for Frank L. VanderSloot, who believed in me as a young adult and gave me my first job working for him at Melaleuca, Inc. Actually, Frank gave me more than a job. He gave me a chance to participate at a level well above what I deserved and gave me a front-row seat to witness the dynamic growth of his company. He gave me a head start in life.

I'm grateful for my editor, Pamela Suarez, for her amazing work and advice; for the content editing added by Professor Vicky Crittenden of Babson College, for my mentor, Jim Northrop, who gave me great insight and constant encouragement. Thanks to Stuart Johnson founder and CEO of Success Partners and Todd Eliason Publisher and Editor in Chief of Direct Selling News for helping improve the accuracy of the data included. I'm also grateful for my oldest daughter Madison for designing this book's cover, and for a Christmas-time discussion with my brothers Brock and Dave, who gave me the final push to stop talking and start interviewing and writing.

Finally, a special thanks for the love, support and patience of my wife and eternal companion, Erin, whom I love, and our children: Spencer and his wife Maris, Madison, Allison, Sydney and Kate. Much of the experience I've gained came at great sacrifice on their part as we moved from Utah to Idaho to Boston to Dallas to Utah to Sydney, Australia to Utah to California to Utah to Arizona to Texas and back to Arizona.

Prologue

The year was 1991. I was a senior at Brigham Young University about to graduate *cum laude* with a degree in business communications. I was wrapping up my tenure as student body president, had recently been named Communications Student of the Year, and was fresh off a summer internship with U.S. Senator Orrin Hatch. I had it all—including an ego the size of my home state of Utah.

I would soon be forced to abandon that ego, however, when the job search I'd been looking forward to with great anticipation didn't pan out quite the way I'd hoped. In fact, it was the opposite of what I'd hoped. As the rejections poured in from company after company, my attitude devolved from cockiness to confusion to denial to outright mortification. I was devasted.

I was sitting at the breakfast table one morning reading the job classifieds when I stumbled across an opening for an entry-level public relations manager at a company I'd never heard of before: Melaleuca, Inc.

"Melaleuca?" I snickered. "That sounds like something you'd cough up during a bad cold!"

Still, a job's a job. I did a little research on Melaleuca, Inc. and learned that it was a relatively young company that sold wellness and household products containing an essential oil called Melaleuca Alternifolia *(Aha! I* thought. *That's where the funny company name comes from!)* Founded in 1985 in Idaho Falls, Idaho, Melaleuca was a fast growing, award-winning global company with a highly-decorated founder/CEO. Everything sounded great, except …

"… it's one of those network marketing companies," I explained to my wife, Erin, later that morning. "You know the kind, where people sell products to their friends and then try to recruit them to become 'distributors'?"

"Oh!" Erin said. "You mean it's a pyramid scheme. Do you really want to work for a company like that?"

"It can't be that bad," I replied. "Melaleuca's got an A-plus rating from the Better Business Bureau. They're expanding like crazy and the CEO is winning awards all over the place for his leadership and business acumen."

"Well," she sighed, patting her belly, "with this baby on the way, we need to do *something*. I guess it can't hurt to check it out."

So, two months later, on a cold and gray November day, I set aside my mammoth ego and, along with my pregnant wife, drove north on Yellowstone Highway to Melaleuca's headquarters on the banks of the Snake River in Idaho Falls for my first on-site interview with founder and CEO Frank VanderSloot.

Erin and I had little interest in moving away from our families in Utah and were more than a tad concerned about working for a network marketing company. To our great surprise, we left Idaho Falls that weekend with not only a job offer, but also a new world view. We, like thousands of others who would hear Frank's vision, were convinced that there was something unique about his company, its products and its mission. We drove back to Utah that Sunday relatively sure we would accept Frank's offer. The next week on the phone, before I officially accepted, I warned Frank of my intentions.

"My plan is to work for two or three years and then apply to Harvard Business School," I said. "Are you okay hiring me knowing I might only be there a few years?"

"Brett, your job will be to do your best to get accepted by Harvard," Frank replied, "and my job will be to convince you that you're better off not going."

Thus, I started my career in direct selling in January of 1992 as Melaleuca's Manager of Public Relations. Although I did leave in 1994 to attend Harvard Business School and earn my MBA, I remain grateful for the full and exciting years working with Frank VanderSloot. Not only did he treat me like a son, but he also allowed me to be part of his senior management team. He gave me assignments typically reserved for executives many years my senior. I became a registered lobbyist; represented the company at civic, government and industry events; learned and led marketing communications; and traveled with Frank and watched as he worked with field leaders, vendors, employees, media, and many other key constituencies. All this during a period of growth that would see the company's sales increase ten times from around $20 million to more than $210 million, and their manufacturing footprint expand beyond Southeastern Idaho with another 100,000 square feet in Knoxville, Tennessee.

What I expected to be a brief opportunity to work alongside a skilled CEO and gain general management experience in preparation for an MBA became a twenty plus-year career that has provided me the chance to live and work around the world. It also put me in the eye of one of the channel's major public relations storms as another up-and-coming direct seller, Nu Skin Enterprises, caught the attention of state regulators and put the entire sales channel under a regulatory microscope for the first few years of my career. Rather than sit back and watch a competitor take a public beating, Frank went on the offense and brought me along to learn. He gave me a front row seat in the battle between consumer protection regulators and direct sellers. Frank reached out to the most aggressive regulators. He asked for in-person meetings and approached them all with the same statement: "We believe we are different than other multi-level marketing companies. We have taken great care to make sure we don't harm consumers, and we want to show you exactly what we're doing and invite you to tell us what—if anything—we need to change."

Frank's "white knight" strategy worked with the regulators. It was backed by a tough self-regulating team inside the company, and it resonated with potential customers and distributors, too. In a time of great uncertainty in the sale channel, Frank's bold approach allowed Melaleuca to continue to grow at breakneck speed.

The management, marketing, and sales experience I gained as part of my close working relationship with Frank, combined with the channel and regulatory context I obtained during our meetings around the country, accelerated my career opportunities after business school. I've been fortunate to carefully select and work with a few of the best network marketing companies: Melaleuca, Beachbody, USANA Health Sciences and AdvoCare; and have had the unique experience of also leading party plan direct selling companies Jewel Kade and Origami Owl Family of Brands. While there are executives out there with more tenure at specific companies, I am unique in the number of direct selling companies I have served in senior executive and/or CEO roles, and one of the few to have worked in both party plan and network marketing companies.

I've worked in both public companies (USANA Health Sciences) and private companies in the U.S. and in Australia, New Zealand, Canada, Mexico, South Korea, Hong Kong, Taiwan, and Japan. I've worked with Fortune 500 companies evaluating direct selling, and several direct selling companies evaluating new markets, new products, and new opportunities. I've worked in high growth companies, led massive turnarounds, and worked with declining companies with scarce resources. I've enjoyed great times and led companies through some of the worst media, regulatory and financial periods you can imagine. Along the way, I've had the opportunity to watch, listen, learn and consult with dozens of investors and financial providers to direct sellers. Through those opportunities I've seen institutional and individual investors make exceptional returns while others suffered catastrophic losses.

Those last two things—the exceptional returns and the catastrophic losses—are the reasons for this book.

The Challenge

In 2005, after several years of serving as an executive in direct selling, I was invited to join a small group of experts who would make themselves available to answer investors' questions about direct selling companies. The pay was good, and they made the calls work with my schedule, so I was happy to participate.

Through that endeavor, I have had dozens of phone calls and face-to-face conversations with investors interested in a direct selling company. For the most part, the professionals I have spoken with have had interesting questions and our discussions were engaging enough to make our hour together zoom by. After several of these calls, I began to understand how to translate my experience into language that could be meaningful and helpful to these investment professionals who had little experience evaluating direct selling companies, and therefore had questions that were informed by the industries they *did* have experience with—most often, retailing. Later, while serving as a board member myself, I witnessed how dangerous it was for directors (and investors) to try and apply retail metrics and know-how to direct selling.

During my calls and conversations with professional investors, I often found myself spending the first thirty minutes setting the context and helping them understand the nuances of the sales channel. That discussion usually led to good questions, but after nearly every phone call I worried that the investment professional, though thorough in their questions, might still lack the core understanding necessary to make a truly educated decision about investing in direct selling companies.

The Solution

That's why I wrote this book. I intend to provide in one handy, accessible guide the background and insight that private equity, debt and venture capital professionals need to effectively evaluate potential investments in direct selling companies. I also hope to help new board members and advisors with no channel experience so that they will be better prepared to contribute. *Private Equity Investing in Direct Selling: Identifying Risk and Rewards* is not conceived as a *New York Times* bestseller. It's written to a narrow audience of institutional and individual investors like you who are considering spending their time or money in a sales channel that is evolving from "direct selling" to "social selling," with so much potential to evolve and grow even further. I believe that growth and the ability to scale the channel beyond the niche it occupies today is more probable if we are successful in attracting the money and the minds of professional capital. My hope is that those who read this guide will become better founders and owners, wiser advisors and board members, and great partners. True success will come when the channel not only attracts more financial capital, but when there are serial institutional investors who enter the arena over and over with a success rate that rivals other commerce-centric industries. That is the outcome I want to help foster.

In the pages that follow, you will learn:

- The various types of direct sellers, and an overview of the direct selling channel as a whole
- How direct sellers are different from typical retailers, and how those differences affect you as an investor and/or advisor
- How to determine if a company is operating under a pyramid scheme

- Why direct selling—and/or many of the techniques used by direct sellers—is destined to explode in the Millennial Age, and how you can capitalize on it
- The specific attributes direct sellers want and expect from their board members, investors and advisors; and concrete ways you can add value when serving in those roles
- A series of due diligence tips that will help you properly evaluate a company's leadership, sales system, regulatory risk, culture, and much more
- How I would and would not invest in a direct selling company

In addition, to augment my experience as a board member and CEO of two companies owned by private equity investors and/or large lenders, I interviewed and share here the insights of nearly thirty CEOs of direct selling's largest companies, with a particular focus on (1) those who are new to direct selling and can compare and contrast it with other industries, (2) those who lead public companies and have considerable experience talking with professional investors, and (3) those who lead companies that are currently or were previously owned by private equity investors, or who have accessed capital markets in significant ways. I also interviewed investment bankers, analysts and private equity partners who have experience in the space, and I impart their wisdom here as well.

Before we dive into the guide, I wish to issue an acknowledgment and a warning: financial analysts might find this book wanting if they are looking for comparables and ratios. While I will give you questions to guide you in your evaluations and a KPI or two to focus on, this book is not intended to be a deep descent into the finer points of evaluating companies financially. My goal is to share 20+ years of my insight along with the acumen of a cadre of experts in an attempt to highlight the opportunities and help you distinguish them from the "here today, gone tomorrow" red herrings that rise and fall so often in our channel.

Let's begin.

The Goal of This Book:

My goal in writing this book is simple: I want to make sure investors benefit from the cash-rich economics of an industry that is evolving into mainstream social selling. When they do, more capital will be available to fund the dreams and social benefits many of our founders started their companies to achieve.

No investor should lose money they have deployed in direct selling, and no founder should continue to believe that their investors' only value is the cash they bring to the table. The industry needs more capital, but even more, it needs the help of smart investors and savvy executives from outside the industry to help close the gap between current practices and those that will help it scale as an industry into the mainstream of public acceptance.

Chapter 1

Why You Can't Ignore Direct Selling

When I began my research for this book, I thought my understanding of direct selling and the scope of its reach was clear. I have worked in or around the channel for more than 25 years. I was invited to serve on the Direct Selling Association's board of directors, been the CEO or GM of four direct selling companies and led marketing and/or communications for two of the largest companies.

Having been so heavily immersed in the direct selling arena for decades, I thought I knew all of the channel's significant companies and the way they worked. I knew that direct selling had found its way through the dark years when pyramid schemes masqueraded as legitimate companies. I knew that the channel had made major progress in working with regulators to improve our self-regulation. In the past decade, I've been delighted to witness a significant realignment behind a common goal of creating consumer value. I knew that the "gig economy" had forever changed direct selling's virtual monopoly on side-hustle opportunities and introduced healthy competition that was driving meaningful changes in legacy companies and inspiring impressive new start-ups with a social-centric approach to product sales and sharing.

That's what I knew. What I failed to understand was how key elements of the channel had been deployed effectively in companies that don't consider themselves to be direct sellers. My eyes were opened with a single call from an executive from the world's largest accounts receivable management and debt collection company. He called to ask for my help in his efforts to renew their salesforce's confidence in their future. This B2B service company had effectively deployed an independent sales force with a multi-level marketing (MLM) compensation system for many years, and through it had developed mainstream clients including several Fortune 100 companies. That phone call—and the subsequent consulting work I did with that company—sparked my interest in how the economics and attributes of direct selling could be applied in different (and quite remarkable) ways across the commercial spectrum. I started looking for more examples of conventional companies leveraging direct selling principles and was rewarded with some interesting new insights. The following are a few direct sellers listed by industry that may surprise you.

Real Estate

Two of the world's fastest growing and most successful real estate brokerage companies employ an MLM compensation plan to pay agents to recruit and mentor other agents: Keller Williams and eXp World Holdings, Inc. In January 2019, eXp announced: "eXp Realty, the first, cloud-based real estate brokerage and a subsidiary of eXp World

Holdings, Inc. (NASDAQ: EXPI), today announced that it surpassed 16,000 agents and brokers in North America, which represents an increase of more than 145 percent since the same time last year."[1] This stunning growth is the result of an MLM compensation plan that turns real estate agents into dedicated evangelists for the brand. Smart!

Financial Services

I knew of the success of Primerica, Inc. (PRI), a life insurance company with 2018 revenues of more than $1.8 billion, but I was surprised to learn that TransAmerica, a $19 billion holding company for various life insurance companies and investment firms, deploys a direct selling model through World Financial Group. Here is how they describe their opportunity on their website: "To give people from all backgrounds the power to become financial services business owners, so that every family can access financial knowledge, products, and resources to prepare for a better future.."[2] With 10,000 baby boomers reaching retirement age every day in America, the financial services industry is ripe for this kind of innovation.

Smoking Cessation

Philip Morris has discovered the power of direct selling and hired one of the channel's leading consulting firms to help them develop out-of-

---

[1] https://www.globenewswire.com/news-release/2019/01/18/1701957/0/en/eXp-Realty-Exceeds-16-000-Real-Estate-Agents-Across-North-America.html, accessed May 9, 2019.

[2] http://worldfinancialgroup.com/learn-about, accessed June 25, 2019

retail, word-of-mouth marketing and sales campaigns to drive adoption of a new smoking cessation product in Eastern Europe. According to my sources, the program produced a 400% increase in sales for the product after just one year. An expansion of the program into new markets began in 2019.

Rideshare Industry

TRYP Technologies, Inc., is launching a competitor to Uber and Lyft with a model that features a flat monthly fee to drivers of $195. The drivers then keep 100% of the fares they collect. TRYP also introduced a points-based social sharing feature to acquire and retain loyal customers. This is how their website explains their multi-level rewards program: "Our platform is built around a community. The TRYP Rides Community is strong, savvy, and its members are constantly rewarded for helping it grow. Our innovative rewards program gives you points EVERY TIME you or one of your referred friends or family uses the app. It's called Frequent TRYP Rides Rewards Program and it's a game-changing way to earn points while you travel."[3] I predict success for this application of direct selling principles to an evolving and highly competitive industry.

Beauty

In the beauty business—one of direct selling's strongest categories— COTY invested $600 million to expand its reach beyond brick-and-mortar retail. Here is how CFO.com described Coty's acquisition:

---

[3] https://www.tryprides.com/ride/tryp-rewards/, accessed May 9, 2019.

Coty is opening up a new channel for distributing beauty products by acquiring control of online peer-to-peer seller Younique for about $600 million.

According to THE WALL STREET JOURNAL, Younique is "part of a crop of upstarts that have taken the direct-selling business model pioneered by companies such as Amway and Avon and adapted it to the internet age."

It employs "presenters" to sell its branded makeup and skin care products directly to consumers through social media. If users buy the products within an allotted time frame, the presenter—often a young mother working from home—receives royalties.[4]

Travel and Entertainment

In the entertainment (and soon, travel) space, VERVE (verve.co) has raised more than $80 million in venture funding for a peer-to-peer marketing platform. CEO and co-founder Callum Negus-Fancey has built an entire event marketing business that helps develop brands by rewarding individuals for word-of-mouth advertising. This is how they describe their business: "We elevate lives by bringing people closer to the things they love. We're the global platform for 16 to 28-year-olds to discover and buy from aspirational brands through their network."[5]

The company is on track to generate $250 million in 2019 (up from a reported $100 million in 2018) and has attracted some of the biggest

---

[4] http://www.cfo.com/ma/2017/01/coty-younique-beauty-products/, accessed May 9, 2019.

[5] https://verve.co/, accessed May 9, 2019.

names in sports, entertainment, and travel as partners, including Marriott, Ticketmaster, MGM Resorts, Front Gate Tickets, Eventbrite, ESPN, and Universal Music Group. All of their success has come without paying out a single dollar in their "compensation plan." Negus-Fancey has instead offered free ticket and VIP experiences to fuel his word-of-mouth marketing engine.

Darren Jensen, CEO of LifeVantage, spoke to Vinayak Hegde, a LifeVantage board member, the former global CMO at Groupon and currently Lead of Global Growth Marketing and Traffic Platform for Airbnb. Jensen left that conversation and concluded, "We have to agree that companies like Uber, Lyft, Amazon, Groupon, or Airbnb have the same goal as direct selling, which is to create entrepreneurs. Hedge told me that the Airbnb mission is essentially to create millions of entrepreneurs. So really, there is no difference between the mission of LifeVantage and that of Airbnb—both companies are creating entrepreneurs. Right now, we're doing it slightly differently, but sometimes they're overlapping with this. We are all competing for the attention of a finite number of entrepreneurs."

Valuable Learning For Other Portfolio Companies

Whether you are planning to invest in a traditional direct selling company or join an advisory board of one of the "gig economy" companies like VERVE, Amazon, Groupon, Uber or Airbnb, this book will help you become a more valuable partner and a wiser investor by sharing with you some of the 100-plus years of learning from the companies that make up the original side hustle industry. When I asked author, speaker, educator and champion of social good Devin Thorpe for his view on the channel, he said that direct selling "… was the beginning of what we now call the gig economy. It was Uber before Uber was Uber. It was Lyft, it was TaskRabbit, it was all these gig economy things, up to and including being a Forbes contributor. That's what this is, except that it has the nobility of offering much more upside. You can't drive Uber enough to get rich, but you can sell enough vitamins to get rich."

Direct Selling is Maturing and Coming of Age

In my interviews with CEOs and at least one professional who has facilitated several transactions, I was told that many professional investors are hesitant to add a direct selling company to their portfolio even though there have been very reputable investors active in later-stage transactions in direct selling. For example, consider what's happened since 2017: TPG made a $1 billion investment in Rodan+Fields for a 25% stake in the company making the valuation north of $3 billion. LNK has announced a successful exit from Beachbody with The Raine Group becoming Beachbody's new PE partner. Coty has invested $600 million in Younique. Arbonne's investors announced an exit in a sale to the French conglomerate Groupe Rocher, and Korean powerhouse LG has reached an agreement to purchase New Avon.

While direct selling has been around for more than 100 years, the channel has yet to become more than a niche player in the world of retail. However, the above investments are evidence that significant consumer trends are driving more and more interest in both direct selling companies and the social commerce techniques the channel uses to facilitate

7

transactions offline and online. While the world has become increasingly more comfortable shopping outside of the retail box and user reviews and references from friends have grown more prominent to purchasers, most companies are struggling to effectively and predictably drive sales through word-of-mouth like direct sellers have done for years.

In an article for SOCIAL SELLING NEWS, writer Teresa Day Craighead interviewed retail consultant Carol Spieckerman, owner of consulting firm Spieckerman Retail. In that article Spieckerman reportedly said, "In retail now, selling direct to the customer is all the rage. It's no longer against the rules for a wholesaler to bypass a department store and go directly to the customer. What was previously seen as a huge threat is now embraced as brand expansion. That's a radical change. Direct sellers are the cool kids now, because everybody's trying to go direct to the customer."[6]

Spieckerman sees the lines continuing to blur between direct sellers and mainstream retailers. "One thing is for sure," she says, "direct to consumer is going to become a bigger tent. Everybody is trying to go into some form of direct sales."[7]

These retail and consumer trends, direct selling's proven success in consumer-to-consumer commerce, and the channel's aggressive effort to eliminate bad actors are signs that direct selling may be a method of distribution whose time has finally come. As an investor, now is the time to consider adding a direct selling company to your portfolio, both to capitalize on the channel's ability to produce three- to five-times returns

---

[6]   https://socialsellingnews.com/features/big-brands-enter-direct-selling-as-pressure-grows/, accessed May 9, 2019.

[7] Ibid.

driven by its impressive cash flows, and also because of the learnings you can acquire and apply to portfolio companies trying to innovate themselves beyond the retail box.

TPG's co-CEO and co-founder Jim Coulter said that their investment in Rodan+Fields was in fact an investment in learning how to apply direct selling techniques. In the press release announcing their investment in Rodan+Fields, Coulter said, "We see Rodan+Fields as being at the intersection of emerging consumer trends and technology disruptions."

Later in this book we will discuss how I believe investors can help direct sellers close the gap that keeps them from becoming more mainstream, but as an investor I think you would be wise to consider what you can learn from the years of direct-to-consumer, socially driven, word-of-mouth marketing that has been a core competency of direct sellers for many years.

On Trend Attributes

We will define direct selling, distinguish it from direct marketing and provide you a numeric overview of the channel in the next chapter, but here is a list a few of the attributes of direct selling that puts the channel at the center of emerging consumer trends and technology:

- 100% Variable Expense Salesforce—no money spent until a sale is made
- No-Risk Marketing and Sales—no capital at risk to 'trigger' transactions
- Leads with a relationship followed by a transaction
- Use of social media and mobile technology to sell and market

- Compensation systems designed to motivate both customer and distributor acquisitions
- Ability to engage the customer in long-format storytelling and education

Uniquely Suited to the Millennial Marketplace

In a 2017 article published by *FORBES.COM*, web and TV personality, bestselling author and CEO of Zen Media, Shama Hyder, articulated the opportunity for direct selling in this way:

Their inherently social model has the potential to make them uniquely suited to a marketplace in which trust, relatability, and a strong network are critical features of a competitive edge ... If direct sales companies can identify real social challenges their service model either solves or simplifies while presenting win-win value propositions, they can join the ranks of those socially-savvy companies, like Lyft, Airbnb and Tom's, that speak 'millennial' fluently.[8]

I believe direct sellers have a model whose time has come and can best "join the ranks" of the "socially-savvy companies," with capital partners who can bring outside expertise to them as advisors and partners. This book is not only designed to demonstrate the value of such a partnership, but to also make sure that you enter the partnership with

---

[8]   https://www.forbes.com/sites/shamahyder/2017/08/14/why-direct-sales-companies-need-to-reach-the-end-consumer/#285750f612a4, accessed May 9, 2019.

eyes wide open and well aware of the nuances that make this channel so unique.

Chapter 2

Direct Selling Overview—Large, Growing and Hidden from Capital Markets

When I started working in the direct selling channel in 1992, consumers purchased their goods from inside the box of brick-and mortar retailers. Most purchases were made via cash or check. Catalogs were well understood but catalog sales made up a relatively small segment of annual consumer retail sales volume, and home delivery and distribution services were under developed and not optimized for quick deliveries.

Times have changed, and brick-and-mortar retailers are struggling for relevance. In fact, the 2018 Deloitte holiday retail survey estimated that online shopping for the 2018 holidays was "expected to account for 57 percent of all purchases."[9]

The technology innovations driving improvements and efficiencies in customer acquisition, targeted marketing, high-information driven decision

---

[9] https://www2.deloitte.com/insights/us/en/industry/retail-distribution/holiday-retail-sales-consumer-survey.html?nc=1, accessed May 20, 2019.

making and the decentralization of shopping has created new and exciting opportunities for investors.

More than at any time in history, investors understand the returns possible when the masses are empowered with easy-to-execute opportunity. Investors live in a world fascinated by Uber and intoxicated by the democratization of opportunity that has powered the domination of commerce by Amazon and the disruption of entertainment by Apple, Netflix, and YouTube. While these changes have warmed institutional capital to looking at new channel opportunities including direct selling, typically the "smart money" financial investors know little about the direct selling and are not aware of the size of some of the companies in the arena. Before I introduce you to the channel's size and to sizeable companies therein, let's define the channel and be clear about what companies are direct selling entities.

What is a "Direct or Social" Selling Company?

According to the Direct Selling Association, "Direct selling is a business model that offers entrepreneurial opportunities to individuals as independent contractors to market and/or sell products and services, typically outside of a fixed retail establishment, through one-to-one selling, in-home product demonstrations or online. Compensation is ultimately based on sales and may be earned based on personal sales and/or the sales of others in their sales organizations."[10]

Social selling is sometimes used as a euphemism for direct selling and a way of modernizing the channel. However, there are companies

---

[10] https://www.dsa.org/, accessed May 20, 2019.

that are deliberate, and deservedly so, about the use of the descriptor. These companies are independent sellers who are attempting to transact more of their sales via social media than via live face-to-face selling experiences.

Direct Selling is Not Direct Marketing

Sometimes it is easier to understand what something is not, before you get clarity about what it is. So, let's start by clearing up common confusions. Many of the analysts I've spoken with are confused and associate direct selling companies with direct marketing companies. Though both channels bypass retailers and go direct to consumers, direct selling and direct marketing are not the same. Direct marketing companies reach consumers via an advertising media, most often a TV infomercial (though this opportunity is becoming less viable as eyeballs have scattered) or a printed or online catalog. The key difference is the requirement for risk capital in direct marketing. Direct marketers have to purchase consumer attention and hope for a sale. Not so with direct selling.

In a report on direct selling in India, KPMG articulated the difference between direct sales and direct marketing in these terms:

The crucial difference between both the methods hinge on the mode of publicity that a firm uses to generate awareness in the market. While Direct Marketing uses one or more advertising mediums, Direct Selling relies on direct engagement with the purchaser to generate a specific response or call to action that can be measured.

Direct Marketing is a type of advertising in which companies communicate directly to the customers through formats like online advertisements, direct mail, text messaging and telemarketing. Direct Selling on the other hand involves marketing and demonstration of a product or service directly to the customer usually through a personal contact/relationship with the salesperson.11

Types of Direct Selling Companies

Traditionally, direct sales companies have been further defined by the compensation system they employ and the method of engaging the consumer. Most direct sales companies define themselves as one of three types:

Door-to-Door

Door-to-door sales is just what its name implies—a method of selling that takes place in person and typically at the home of the potential buyer. Door-to-door sales companies compensate sellers by paying them commissions on the seller's personal sales. While there are several companies that still use door-to-door sales, especially "summer sales" in the pest control, roofing and home services industries, most of these companies are NOT included in traditional direct selling statistics. In fact, the type of door-to-door selling previously utilized by Fuller Brush and Encyclopedia Britannica is rarely used by today's direct sellers.

---

[11]   https://assets.kpmg/content/dam/kpmg/pdf/2014/12/Direct-Selling.pdf, accessed May 20, 2019

Large ticket items like vacuum cleaners, cookware, roofs, and annual contracts for services can all be sold effectively through door-to-door sales because the model allows sufficient margin to pay large commissions to reward a salesperson for persisting amid the mostly "not interested" responses they get.

Since the 80s, several companies have created successful summer sales programs that utilize college students to sell books, cable TV and telecommunications services, roofing, insulation, bug and rodent treatment, and solar energy.

While door-to-door sales continue to be looked upon as a costly and inefficient way to reach consumers, there is at least one example of a company that has used this model to create significant value. Most recently, door-to-door seller Vivint turned heads by selling to Blackstone for $2 billion. Blackstone saw in Vivint a company that had mastered the art of door-to-door sales by creating a model that turned one-time sales into recurring revenue streams from security alarm monitoring and servicing. Shortly after acquiring Vivint, the company opened Vivint Solar as a separate (now public) company that generated a reported $1.1 billion return for Blackstone.

Person-to-person (Network Marketing/MLM)

Person-to-person direct selling primarily compensates individuals for building a team of personal consumers. Because the commissions on the individual items sold via this method are typically relatively low per hour of time required to make the sale, it relies on a "multi-level" compensation system that rewards a seller a small amount on sales made by others several layers deep on a team. For example, if John sponsors Tim, Tim would be level/layer one to John. If Tim sponsors Jill, Jill would be John's second level/layer. If one values their time on a dollar-per-hour basis, the economics work for individual sellers only if their customers stay and purchase the product multiple times (thus consumable products are most often sold via person-to-person sales), or if they find others who are both consuming and selling the product to other customers. This ability to leverage time by being compensated for sales made by others, is a key principle used to encourage others to participate. Because the compensation system is so central to the success of this type of direct selling, companies that utilize this method of selling are often referred to as multi-level marketing or MLM companies. However, MLM is more accurately used to describe a characteristic of a compensation system. Using MLM to describe person-to-person sellers can sometimes be confusing since almost all direct sellers, no matter their method of selling, employ compensation systems with the ability to earn commission on multiple levels of salespersons on a team.

Most of the largest companies in the channel are person-to-person direct sellers, and most of these large companies will be found selling consumable goods such as skin care, nutritional supplements, and home cleaning products.

This model of direct selling has attracted bad actors through the years that have given the channel a black eye and continues to fuel negative media coverage. Reputable companies have used their membership in the Direct Selling Association (DSA) to join forces to more strongly regulate the channel. In an article published in February 2019, the Consumer Protection Review wrote of these efforts:

> The Direct Selling Association (DSA) launched the Direct Selling Self-Regulatory Council (DS-SRC), a new enforcement agency charged with policing the direct selling industry. The DS-SRC will be administered by the Advertising Self-Regulatory Council, which operates under the Council of Better Business Bureaus.
>
> Direct selling companies use independent sellers to market and sell products and services, typically outside of a fixed retail establishment. One form of direct selling that has received significant scrutiny from the Federal Trade Commission (FTC) is multilevel marketing (MLM), which distributes products or services through a network of independent salespeople who earn income from their own retail sales and from retail sales made by their direct and indirect recruits.
>
> While the DSA has had a reactive, self-regulatory program for its members for many years, the creation of the DS-SRC appears to be in direct response to FTC commissioners' comments encouraging further self-regulation in the industry and the industry's sometimes negative public perception.[12]

Network marketing is different from the other two types of direct selling in that it de-emphasizes selling and focuses participants on creating residual earnings. Network marketing companies teach

---

[12] https://www.consumerprotectionreview.com/2019/02/proactive-self-regulatory-council-direct-selling-industry-launches-january/, accessed May 20, 2019.

representatives to sell subscription-like recurring orders to customers, and because companies offer discounts to representatives, many customers enroll as distributors whether or not they intend to sell for the purpose of securing a 10-25% discount on their monthly product order.

Most network marketing companies sell consumable products that require monthly replenishment such as vitamins, personal care items and most recently energy and telecommunications services. The high re-order rate among these companies creates attractive economics for the distributors who earn over and over on a one-time sale to a customer. These subscription-like re-orders are also the bread and butter of many network marketing companies that typically have more than 75% of their revenue coming from recurring sales.

Traditionally, network marketing companies were known for distributors' tendency to focus on "selling the opportunity" rather than on selling the product itself. Distributors who practice this method of business development argue that there are more people who need extra income than need a specific product. They argue that if they can convince potential customers to become distributors, they will also become a product consumer. As they enroll more distributors, their time spent is leveraged and they get both a customer (product purchaser) and another team member helping them sell (remember that distributors earn overrides on sales made by those on their team). The tendency to lead with opportunity is becoming an outdated practice and more of the recent network marketing success stories include companies that have much more of a product sales focused approach.

Network marketing include companies like Nu Skin, USANA Health Sciences, Herbalife, Beachbody, Morinda, Modere, Nature's Sunshine, Melaleuca, Inc., and Neora (formerly Nerium).

Party Plan

Not to be confused with a "party planner" or a company that plans parties, party plan companies are known for in-home demonstrations and product sales. Party plan companies employ a one-to-group selling system vs a one-to-one approach. These companies have traditionally struggled in urban markets where space is a premium and people tend to live in small apartments rather than larger homes. The model still does quite well in rural America where retail options are relatively scarce. Party plan companies tend to have large followings in the Ohio River Valley, in the Midwest and in the central valley of California. Party plan companies pay higher retail commissions on personal sales and have a multi-level compensation system to reward sellers for recruiting others to sell and for training those they recruit.

The party plan model of direct selling has been dominated by women selling jewelry, make-up, home decor, kitchen utensils, and personal care items. Some of the well-known party plan companies are Pampered Chef (acquired by Berkshire Hathaway)[13], Tupperware, Thirty-One Gifts, Scentsy, Home Interiors, Southern Living at Home, and Princess House.

Party plan sellers are compensated at a rate of between 20-50% of each retail sale made, and those who recruit others to sell can earn

---

[13] http://www.berkshirehathaway.com/news/sep2302.html, accessed June 26, 20

residual overrides of between 5-15% on others. In early days, leaders would earn residual just on those they recruited, but it is more common today for companies to offer a multi-level compensation plan that rewards leaders on sales made up to ten levels deep in their organization. Top party plan sellers earn anywhere between $300,000 and $1.2 million per year.

While the party plan model continues to be a popular choice for many entrepreneurs, and there continue to be examples of companies generating between $50 million and $800 million in sales, the model has struggled to produce more than one billion-dollar company (Mary Kay who many would argue is not a party plan company) and to maintain companies with sales of more than $500 million.

Regardless of the model a company uses, the unifying characteristic of the channel is the use of independent (IRS form 1099) sellers that are not on payroll, are paid only when products are sold, and are relied on to deliver most of the sales and marketing activities. While we call these 1099 representatives by multiple names, almost all companies rely on them to do the bulk of the advertising, customer acquisition, selling, product education, some customer service and the recruiting and training of others to do the same. According to the DSA:

Direct sellers may be called distributors, representatives, consultants or various other titles. They may participate in various ways, including selling the products themselves or through their sales organizations, providing training and leadership to their sales organizations, referring customers to the company and purchasing products and services for personal use.[14]

Other Companies of Note

Avon, one of the largest and oldest direct-selling companies, is not listed in either of the models above because of their unique combination of full-time field leadership, high-turn sellers and the use of retail locations and catalogs as the primary sales triggers. While Avon has added a multilevel compensation plan that has reportedly made up a significant percent of the company's volume, their model is sufficiently different to classify them more as a stand-alone direct selling hybrid. Also, there are up and coming companies that are pioneering new ways of using social media to transact sales. Beachbody, known for their infomercial brands such as Insanity and P90X, has evolved from a traditional network marketing company to a company that transacts nearly 70% of all of its network marketing revenue from social media interactions led by their distributors. Younique has grown to more than $40 million a month in revenue from several countries with a sales model that relies on virtual parties, primarily on Facebook.

---

[14] https://www.dsa.org/, accessed May 20, 2019.

Direct Selling by the Numbers

According to an article published by THE DIRECT SELLING NEWS:

>It was another record year for the direct selling industry, which garnered $192.9 billion (constant U.S. dollars) in estimated retail sales globally in 2018—a 1.2 percent increase over 2017—and produced 24 billion Dollar Markets, according to research by the World Federation of Direct Selling Associations (WFDSA), its partner DSA and direct selling companies around the world.[15]

In the latest statistical report, the DSA tallied $34.9 billion in estimated retail sales for 2017 in the United States.[16] According to the World Federation of Direct Selling, the Asia-Pacific region is the site of the largest share of global sales in the direct selling market, with 46%. For the first time, China became the largest direct selling country in 2018 though the WFDSA declared a tie for first place given the fact that their numbers included some estimates and the reported differences were so small. Here are the 2018 top direct selling markets as ranked by sales in USD:

- China ($35.7 billion)
- United States ($35.4 billion)
- Korea ($18. billion)
- Germany ($17.5 billion)
- Japan ($15.6 billion)
- Brazil ($10.2 billion)
- Mexico ($5.9 billion)

---

[15] Direct Selling News, August 2019
[16] 2018 Growth & Outlook Report: U.S. Direct Selling in 2017

- France ($5.4 billion)
- Malaysia ($5.3 billion)
- Taiwan, China ($3.9 billion)[17]

Individual Direct Sellers

In the August 2019 issue, the *DIRECT SELLING NEWS* sited recently published WFDSA 2018 statistics in reporting:

> *The industry's global sales force reached 118.4 million, up 1.6 percent over 2017. Since 2015, more than 13.8 million more individuals have joined the ranks. New sales force segmentation data shows 10.5 million full-time (30+ hours weekly), 42.9 million part-time (up to 30 hours weekly)*

Nearly 16% of all US households have a direct selling representative in the home. Direct selling is a predominantly female business: 74% of all representatives are women, three of four are married, and about 50% have a child under the age of 18 in the home.[18]

Direct Selling Public Companies

While many professional investors and capital lenders find it difficult to list many privately held direct selling companies (for reasons I will discuss in a moment), most can name at least a few of the public direct selling companies like Avon and Tupperware. Here is a list of the top five public companies as measured by market cap on the April 18, 2019[19]:

[17] WORLD FEDERATION OF DIRECT SELLING IN 2018, ESTIMATED RETAIL
[18] https://wfdsa.org/global-statistics/, accessed May 20, 2019.

Company (Market Cap):

- Herbalife Nutrition ($6.156 billion)
- Primerica ($5.12 billion)20
- Nu Skin Enterprises ($2.7 billion)
- Avon Products ($1.777 billion)
- USANA Health Sciences ($1.7 billion)

Top Ten Direct Selling Companies[21]

The list of the top ten direct selling companies is an even mix of public and private companies based on 2018 global revenue (as reported by *Direct Selling News*). The top ten direct selling companies (public and private) listed with their 2018 annual sales numbers are:

- Amway ($8.8B)
- Herbalife ($4.9B)
- Infinitus ($4.5B)
- Vorwerk ($4.3B)
- Natura ($3.67B)
- Coway ($2.5B)
- Tupperware ($2B)
- Young Living ($1.9B)
- Oriflame Cosmetics ($1.55B)

---

[19] http://www.businessforhome.org, accessed June 24, 2019.
[20] NOTE: Primerica does not consider itself a direct selling company
[21] NOTE: Companies that did not report but allegedly have similar sales include Melaleuca, Inc. (~$2B), Mary Kay (~$4B) and doTERRA (~$2+B).||

- Rodan+Fields   ($1.5B)

In total there were 24 companies with more than one billion dollars in global sales in 2017, and a similar number in 2018.[22]

Many investors worry that the direct selling model is not sustainable, and yet there are plenty of companies on the top 100 list that have had sustained sales for decades. Avon (1886) and Vorwerk (1882) are the oldest companies on the list with a history extending back more than 100 years, but many others have been around for decades as well. For example, Tupperware was founded in 1946, Amway celebrated 60 years in 2019, Mary Kay was founded in 1963, Herbalife in 1980, Nu Skin in 1984 and USANA Health Sciences in 1991.

The channel has produced a few companies that have been darlings of the media like Mary Kay, Rodan+Fields, doTERRA, and Stella & Dot. There have also been a few that have had noteworthy private equity transactions like Beachbody, Ruby Ribbon, Arbonne International and PartyLite Candles. Unfortunately, there have also been a few companies that have abused the model, and though most people can't recall the names of those companies because of their obscurity, their collective actions have left a cloud over the channel.

With so many large companies and many with decades of significant sales, why is it so difficult for most professional investors to recall direct selling companies? Only a few like Avon, Beachbody and Rodan+Fields have invested in brand building marketing to drive awareness of their brand, so you don't learn of these companies via media. Nor do you have

---

[22] *DSN* Global 100

direct selling companies making the rounds to introduce themselves to lenders and investors. As we'll discuss in a later chapter, direct selling companies have extremely favorable economic engines with a very high return on invested capital. They have no brick-and-mortar upfront costs as part of the distribution channel, and no at-risk marketing capital required, so most direct selling companies need very little capital at start-up or to scale. With their favorable cash flows, there are very few direct selling companies that have a need to access capital markets. Thus, those who make a living in capital markets will seldom have the chance to take a close look at a direct selling company.

Direct selling is a large and steadily growing sales channel with an underdeveloped capital markets relationship and the lack of awareness of the space has kept many investors from deals that should get done. Consider this example from one investment banker with significant experience in direct selling who told me, "We called more than two hundred private equity firms for a company that was growing by fifty percent and dropping eighteen percent to the bottom line. The company competes in the nutritional space, with a lot of science behind their product, but we could get absolutely no traction even though it was a one hundred-twenty million business, and profitable."

Ultimately, he crafted a deal with a Mexican private equity firm and an operator he knew. This investor and operator doubled the size of the company in less than two years after their acquisition and the investment banker said, "This deal has been one of the most successful this firm has had, but we couldn't get a single PE firm to look at it in the U.S." I called to get an update on this company prior to publishing and learned that the investors have received a 2x return on their capital and the company's rate of growth continues to increase.

For those of you who have invested in direct selling and had disappointing returns, or for those who have heard rumors of others losing money in the channel, I assure you that there are plenty of examples of very solid returns. In the chapters that follow, I will pique your interest in direct selling and improve the odds that any deal you do will generate the above average returns the economics of direct selling companies should produce. Let's get started.

Chapter 3

The Economics of Direct Selling

Most investors become interested in direct selling after they have a chance to examine the economics of this cash rich model of sales and distribution. Long time channel expert and Wall Street researcher Scott Van Winkle wrote, "Successful companies in the channel should generate a higher free cash flow yield given the limited need for fixed capital investment, the higher margin potential as well as what is generally a more attractive working capital model given centralized distribution. With centralized distribution, inventory should turn faster and thus working capital should be more efficient. The attractive financial model characteristics inherent in direct selling have attracted greater investor interest."[23]

I asked Travis Ogden, the CEO of Isagenix and an executive who found his way into direct selling after a successful start in public accounting, why investors should be interested in direct selling.

---

[23]   https://www.directsellingnews.com/june-2012-direct-sellings-efficiency-as-a-business-method-an-analysts-perspective/, accessed May 20, 2019.

"[Direct selling] is an awesome channel when done right," he said. "This business model is phenomenal in terms of the margins it can provide, the cash flow is incredibly healthy, the opportunity to scale quickly, exponential growth and expand across borders is exciting. So, there are so many reasons why this channel makes sense for investing."

As a former CEO of several companies, both direct selling and other channel companies, Jim Northrop has a unique perspective. In the past eight years, Jim has been a consultant to direct selling companies and has guided seven companies through a financial transaction.

When asked about private equity's interest in the direct selling, Jim said, "They are initially interested because of the cash flow dynamics primarily and looking at the high EBITDA rates relative to sales. There's some sort of respect and mystery about the space for financial investors because when they're exposed to those financial results they say, 'Wow, how did they do that?' and their immediate next question is, 'Is that sustainable, or simply an anomaly?'"

In this chapter, we will talk more about the financial dynamics that make professional investors say, "Wow!" and follow with several chapters designed to help you choose those companies with sustainable economics.

Higher Free Cash Flow Yields

Investors who begin to analyze a direct selling company are initially impressed with the cash flow yields of well-run companies. Direct selling companies provide investors many strong liquidity options because they have relatively low capital requirements despite the amount of cash they produce. The high cash flow yields are driven by two factors:

- **High Gross Margins**
- **Low Capital Requirements**

High Gross Margins

Great cash flows start with great margins, and a scan of the top publicly traded direct selling companies (Nu Skin, Avon, Medifast, Herbalife, USANA Health Sciences, and Mannatech) shows gross margins above 70% for all but Avon and above 80% for the nutrition companies. Not only are the margins high and sustainable, but when compared with brick-and-mortar retailing there is very little capital expenditures required of the cash generated by those high margins .

Low Capital Requirements

More often than not, public direct selling companies tend to pay healthy dividends or have an ongoing stock buyback program, because the model doesn't require significant capital reinvestment. For example, unlike traditional retailers, direct sellers **don't require significant investment in brick-and-mortar.** They only need real estate for a relatively lean corporate team and a distribution facility (some choose to manufacture, and many outsource both manufacturing and fulfillment). Beyond the occasional addition of space as the company grows in the U.S. or expands to new countries, there are no retail leases required, no large research and development upfront costs and no significant investments required in specialty manufacturing. In fact, most direct selling businesses started with only capital for inventory and were able to grow with cash from the business—sometimes that growth turned into hundreds of millions of dollars of sales in the first five years—all without a need to access capital markets.

Take Origami Owl as an example. As a 14-year old teenager, Bella Weems decided to sell lockets and charms to earn money to purchase a car when she turned 16. "Weems asked her parents to match the $350 she'd earned for babysitting, which she then spent on wholesale components to make her lockets. She quickly leveraged her network of friends to find buyers." Bella and her mom Chrissy started selling her product at house parties and boutiques and selling at any jewelry show we could. In 2010 she opened a kiosk at the Chandler, Arizona mall in time for Black Friday shoppers.

The Weems didn't have the $7,000 to pay for the mall kiosk, so they contacted a friend Tyson Basha and asked if he would invest. That investment paid off. Sales from the Kiosk generated so much follow-on demand for their product that the Weems decided to start a party plan direct selling company. They began to recruit friends to be their first distributors, and capital to launch. Shawn Maxwell, a Phoenix firefighter and family friend, invested his' life savings,' and Tyson put in more money. As co-founders, Bella Weems, Chrissy Weems, Shawn Maxwell, and Tyson Basha started Origami Owl, one of the fastest-growing direct selling companies in history.

Sales grew and left the family, playing catch-up for the next three years. A company reportedly started with less than $100,000 in capital by a 14-year old and her mother, grew to more than $200 million in the next three years with cash generated by the business. They only sought outside capital when they decided to clean up their cap table and try to get help in upgrading their management.

Direct selling companies are not the only ones that require very little brick-and-mortar. Online and direct marketing companies have similar economic advantages. These two channels, however, typically require an investment in advertising with no assurance that the message or media will trigger the desired transaction. Direct selling companies **require no "at-risk" marketing or advertising capital** because they rely on their representatives to contact and communicate with potential customers. No cash is spent to acquire these representatives. In fact, they only become an expense to the company if and when a transaction is complete. For most direct selling companies, commissions for sales are paid up to a month from the date the sale is made. There is no cash put at risk to generate a product sale.

Some direct sales companies, like Avon, Herbalife and AdvoCare, have chosen to spend money on advertising, but their choice to invest in advertising and sponsorships that would increase brand awareness came years after the companies were producing significant annual cash flow. In other words, advertising and marketing might benefit a direct sales company, but there is no need to put capital at risk to generate sales and produce meaningful cash flows.

To be clear, we are not arguing that there is no capital risk for direct selling companies. Some founders want to have software customized for their business which will require at-risk capital; others might raise money for office space, to build out their team in advance of a launch, and some might even suggest some advertising spend, but history argues that these investments are discretionary and not required for success.

What is required for success is inventory, and for most companies, **inventory is where the bulk of risk capital is deployed**. Unlike retail models where a company can significantly control their rate of growth by controlling the number of distribution points they build or service, direct selling grows via word-of-mouth with no good options for controlling the rate of growth at a corporate level. Because most direct selling representatives are not professional business operators, experience shows that they do not respond well to out-of-stock situations. When they have made a sale and that sale cannot be honored by the company, representatives feel embarrassed and feel like the company has put their reputation at risk. Their response is often to quit and do something else.

Most direct sellers believe they can "never run out," and because there is no way to accurately forecast the demand for a product, they tend to over-invest in inventory at launch. With so few variables available to inform an accurate forecast, direct sellers tend to have the biggest challenge predicting demand at launch or keeping up with hypergrowth just as their "hockey stick" takes a sharp turn north.

For example, one company tapped into hypergrowth when one of its distributors found a very compelling way to do a social media demonstration of a product that previously had years of steady sales. Suddenly, the company experienced a run on this product, and it went out of stock. Meanwhile, other distributors copied the social media demo and demand for the product continued to grow. Unable to keep up with demand, the company was forced to regulate customer orders and stopped receiving new distributor applications. During this time, they introduced a waiting list for those who wanted to become a distributor. The news of the product selling out combined with the waiting list announcement flamed demand, and the company reportedly ended the year with sales of about three-quarters of a billion dollars (more than 300% growth).

The waiting list grew to more than 90,000 people (about five times their current active distributor base) and the company did their best to respond and predict future demand. To their credit, the company made a significant investment in inventory and operation including additional manufacturing capacity. Not knowing what the productivity of those waiting list distributors would be, the company decided to invest in inventory to cover about three times their current run rate (consistent with the growth they had seen that year). When the company's supply issues were resolved, the waiting list went away, there were no longer stock-outs, and the enthusiasm settled closer to two times their original run rate. The company was left with an overstock of inventory.

This scenario is not unique to this company and continues to be a significant challenge for direct sellers. As I write this book, one of my clients is more than 45 days past the launch of a new product that sold out in less than five hours despite what they considered to be an extra bullish inventory purchase. They have continued to struggle to keep the product in stock as new batches are sold in hours or a few days. While excess demand seems to be a great problem to have, this company is losing distributors who have lost confidence in the company's ability to service the sales these distributors are making to people they know (their friends and family).

There are two sides to the inventory coin. Lost sales and upset distributors and customers are one side of the equation. On the other hand, when a company is stuck with inventory there is no easy way to liquidate the product. Given the channel exclusivity demanded by distributors, there are no liquidators, and nowhere to blow it out.

Because of the probability of unpredictable demands along with the lack of solutions to liquidate excess product, inventory risk continues to be the biggest cash challenge the channel faces.

Fortunately, companies that have steady growth typically do have a fairly efficient use of their capital because most direct sellers have a single point of order fulfillment. There is not additional risk in projecting inventory levels in dozens or hundreds of stores or even a handful of distribution centers. Inventory is in one or two warehouses without the risk that comes with significant logistics.

It's important to acknowledge that Amazon's Prime program is putting pressure on direct sellers who have single warehouses (especially those located anywhere other than the central U.S.) and take more than two or three days to get a product to the end consumer. This pressure might require companies to increase their points of distribution to a few at first, and if Walmart and other Amazon competitors continue to improve delivery times, to more retail-like distribution points in the future. The alternative will be to figure out how to absorb upcharges for more rapid delivery services.

Opportunities to Improve Cash Returns

Despite the characteristically strong EBITDA produced by most direct sellers, you will find that most companies could be even more efficient if the out-of-the-channel best practices were deployed in three areas:

- **Technology Productivity Gains**
- **Supply Chain Productivity Gains**
- **Improved Access to Capital**

Technology Productivity Gains

Unlike so many of the venture-backed tech stars, many of the direct selling success stories have had little or no professional stakeholders helping to mature processes and systems. Founders with limited previous business experience find themselves with large and growing companies and while some are fortunate to have hired help along the way, most companies can benefit from the margin enhancements that come from implementing operations and technology discipline.

Direct selling has a unique set of requirements for technology partners due to channel-specific compensation systems. These elaborate compensation programs have given rise to several tech companies that have developed software to accommodate direct sellers. Traditionally, these software companies have tried to provide end-to-end enterprise solutions with order entry, online storefronts, customer service, accounting, and warehouse management. Given the relatively small size of the channel and the scope of the challenges these solutions were addressing, companies have found all but the genealogy and compensation modules to be inferior to other solution specific software. But it has been a painful migration to integrate the best of breed software solutions with legacy compensation software. Most older companies have found that their direct selling solutions leave companies with significant challenges in their effort to implement best of breed technologies for order fulfillment and inventory management, call center and CRM, social and e-commerce. Traditionally, direct selling companies lack many of the tools that drive significant improvements in customer conversion online and rapid improvements in productivity in operations.

Many pre-capital direct selling companies will benefit from technology enhancements that can drive productivity gains.

Supply Chain Productivity Gains

Many direct selling companies have opportunities to improve their margins by improving efficiency all along the supply chain. Typically, direct sellers have failed to invest in forecasting tools that could reduce their inventory on hand and allow them to benefit from discounts (i.e. freight, raw ingredients, etc.) available to those with proper planning. Some have outdated or small-batch manufacturing in-house and others have never revisited their raw ingredient contracts and costs despite significantly higher volumes being purchased.

Many direct selling companies are struggling to meet today's customer demands for fast fulfillment time. While most do an excellent job filling orders in less than 24 business hours, most lack the infrastructure to get anywhere close to the Amazon Prime inspired expectation of 48-hour fulfillment nationwide. Too often direct selling customers are forced to wait a week or more to receive their product.

Improved Access to Capital

Direct sellers continue to be considered a greater-than-average risk to capital markets so profitable direct selling businesses with strong cash flows have been denied access to debt on reasonable terms. Lenders tend to deny or take longer to approve merchant processing services and credit facilities, and when they do offer debt, lenders often charge direct sellers higher rates or offer them terms that require high cash deposits. Profitable direct selling companies have been strapped with deposit requirements that are close to the amount of the debt facility they are seeking. For example, one very well-known direct seller, with ample cash flow and 70% year-to-year growth, was offered a $25 million line of credit with terms that required them to maintain a $25 million cash reserve on deposit with the lender.

Capital markets continue to show a hesitancy to embrace direct selling. Fortunately, most direct sellers enjoy economics that allow them to grow with cash from operations. However, most companies have a need for debt even during the best of times and having the financial flexibility of debt and efficient merchant fees from credit card processors can improve performance.

The lack of interest in each other has combined to make direct sellers more and more foreign to capital market decision makers. The chapters that follow attempt to provide lenders and investors with more information so they can make better decisions and reduce the risk that accompanies partnering with those who choose to build companies with fatal flaws. In the meantime, direct selling companies can benefit from investors with relationships that can improve both their access to capital and their ability to negotiate favorable terms for that capital.

With such outstanding economics built into the sales model and the opportunity to pick up even further margin enhancements with the discipline and guidance of experienced investors, direct selling should be the envy of capital markets. Instead, the channel has had mixed results with some winners, several losers and a reputation for being high risk. The following chapters are designed to provide the investor suggestions on where to focus their due diligence so that they gather enough insight to be able to reduce risk. Investors who follow these guidelines (summarized at the end of Chapter 7) will be able to better identify the companies that will grow to several billion and be around for decades and avoid taking needless risks on companies that are not built to last.

Chapter 4

Common Characteristics of Great Direct Selling Companies

Before we go into depth about specific suggestions of items that should be evaluated during due diligence, it might be helpful to understand the characteristics of the enduring direct or social selling companies. In my twenty-plus years of experience, I have learned that great companies consistently deliver on what I call the "Five S's of Direct Selling:"

- **Social Benefits**—they have more than just an economic reason for being.
- **Stakeholder Value**—they deliver value not only to shareholders, but to all stakeholders including customers, distributors, employees and owners.
- **Sellers Who Add Value**—they have thought through the role of their sellers and positioned them as guides who add value to the customer's experience.

- **Simple Sales System**—they have a straightforward system that causes the newest seller to say, "I can do that!"
- **Stickiness**—they have built attractive hooks into their business so that customers and sellers want to stick around.

Let's discuss each of these Five S's in detail.

Social Benefits

Though it is improving among millennials, direct selling just can't seem to shake the reputation of being a little shady. Some are annoyed by the fact that many direct selling representatives try to recruit their family and friends. Others tell stories of distributors who used bait and switch tactics to get an audience or failed to reveal the true name of the company behind the opportunity they were presenting. Even though these tactics are rarely used by mainstream companies today and more companies are recruiting only after customers have already fallen in love with their products, there is still a need to legitimize the channel and the companies that employ a direct sales force. Great direct selling companies have learned how important it is to engage in social causes that offer a counterpoint to the negative sentiment their distributors often face. Some companies select a cause as an afterthought while others actually form their business around a social cause.

Direct sellers typically deliver social benefits in one or more of the following three ways:

Products that Benefit Society

Beachbody's direct selling division, known as Team Beachbody, has grown to be nearly a billion-dollar enterprise by effectively evangelizing their role in reversing the country's epidemic of obesity. Team Beachbody distributors, called "Coaches," take great pride in their role of helping customers lose weight and improve their health. Beachbody Coaches feel part of something that benefits their customers, their communities and their country and it has nothing to do with supporting a non-profit or charitable cause.

Great direct selling companies are effective in creating a cause around their products. Some companies improve health; others help customers avoid toxins, allergens, carcinogens, or pollutants. Companies that effectively communicate the social benefits of their products often generate significant loyalty and stickiness that improves retention and emboldens sellers with a confidence and passion that prospects respond to with a purchase. These also help to inoculate their distributors and make them more resistant to the naysayers who make negative remarks about being part of an MLM.

Personal Development for Sellers

One of the channel's best-known colloquialisms defines direct selling companies as "personal development companies disguised as a (skin care, nutrition, etc.) company." Most great companies have learned that investing in the personal development of their sales force not only improves productivity, it also increases loyalty. Often salesforce surveys show that distributors who have made little or no income remain loyal to

43

the company and continue to purchase because of the personal development and community the company offers them.

Personal development is a natural outgrowth of being forced to try new things. Direct sellers are only successful if they learn to make new friends, start discussions with strangers, make a product presentation, teach and train others, and speak in public. Engaging in these actions are the beginning of creating opportunities for sellers to grow, but purposeful programs designed to increase the rate of personal growth is what sets great companies apart.

In the 1980s and 1990s, Amway's sales leaders forever changed our channel by making personal development the cornerstone of their sales and recruiting. Top leaders created a culture of daily personal development asserting that every distributor should listen to one motivational or training tape every day. For some of these top leaders, selling training tapes and hosting training events became a much larger money-maker than their Amway product-selling business. According to one Diamond Distributor, some of the top Amway leaders were making less than $500,000 from the products their organizations were selling, but the revenues from the training companies they owned reported income in the tens of millions of dollars. Amway eventually shut down these training companies, but the tradition of offering training, motivation and personal development has continued in many great companies and most offer the content at or below their cost.

Connecting to a Cause Consumers Care About

For the past twenty years, no company has been more closely aligned with the fight against breast cancer than Avon through the company's Avon Products Foundation. Recognizing a need to increase distributor loyalty and seeing "the emerging strategy of linking a company with a cause," Avon's CEO "talked about a new strategy he had heard about, cause-marketing," saying, "Let's explore this."[24] That discussion, reported in 2008 in an article by marketing firm Cone, Inc., was the genesis of a long and effective campaign of connecting Avon and all it thousands of saleswomen to a cause that touches everyone. Avon's employees and salesforce pride themselves in being part of saving lives through education.

Great direct sales companies, especially those who struggle to connect their product directly to a worthwhile cause, have found a way to rally their organizations. Make-up direct seller Younique created The Younique Foundation, an organization committed to providing healing to adult survivors of childhood sexual abuse. Though not tied directly to a specific charity, Thirty-One Gift's foundation, called "Thirty-One Gives" has donated $100 million in product and cash to charitable organizations that share its mission.[25] The Mary Kay Foundation has "granted nearly $74 million to organizations fighting cancer and violence against women."[26]

---

[24] https://www.charitywatch.org/charitywatch-articles/avon-raises-awareness-for-its-cosmetics-and-for-breast-cancer/51, accessed May 20, 2019.
[25] https://www.mythirtyone.com/us/en/info/our-story, accessed May 20, 2019.
[26] https://www.marykayfoundation.org/causes, accessed May 20, 2019.

In Austin, Texas, founder Jessica Honegger has created Noonday Collection as a for-profit social enterprise. Noonday Collection describes their business in these terms: "To make a difference in some of the world's most vulnerable communities, we partner with Artisan Businesses that share our passion for building a flourishing world. We develop these businesses through fair trade, empowering them to grow sustainably and to create dignified jobs for people who need them." In other words, Noonday Collection curates and develops artisans in third world countries and then creates a market for their products with independent sellers in the United States. Jessica believes that "fashion can create connection between women all around the world. And combining fashion with hospitality is a powerful way to engage our communities and create opportunity around the world."[27]

While supporting a cause is not unique to direct selling, the value of cause marketing is critical in not only increasing employee pride and engagement and engendering customer loyalty, but also serving as a social "salve," if you will, in helping distributors heal from the jabs that often come from friends and family as they build their direct selling business.

Stakeholder Value

While the economics of direct selling are attractive most of the time, there are some products and services that are enough of a commodity that they just can't support a commissioned sales force. Great direct selling products deliver value to all stakeholders, but they start by making

---

[27] https://www.noondaycollection.com/about/our-story/, accessed May 23, 2019.

sure their customers are satisfied and feel like they are not overpaying. They deliver customer value and still leave room to pay 20 to 40% in commissions to the sales force, and above-average value for the enterprise and its shareholders.

There are examples of successful utility direct sellers like Stream Energy and Ambit Energy, but in the early days some utility companies came on the scene and drove significant revenues despite the fact that they were competing in a highly commoditized industry. Only after close review did it become evident that there wasn't enough value to pay commissions on the revenues from product sales. Instead, the company created "training programs and fees" that produced the revenue used to pay commissions to the sales force, a practice that turns the company into a pyramid scheme subject to regulatory oversight.

When I asked Bouncer Schiro, CEO of Stream Energy, how he was able to build such a successful energy company, he said it was all about delivering value.

"You have to be relevant," he said. "And if your product isn't relevant at a fair price point, your business will be doomed sooner or later. The only reason Ambit, ACN and Stream are still in business is because we are competitive. And we had to fit a compensation plan into our competitive landscape."

Stream competes in a category in which most direct sellers would hate to do business. Most successful direct selling companies operate in less commoditized product categories where they have the opportunity to distinguish their product with features and benefits customers want, even if they are sold at premium prices. Typically, a company will be required to mark up their product eight to 12 times to sustain the margins necessary to support a typical sales force commission.

Investors should validate the company's value proposition and proceed with caution if the products are not distinctive enough to warrant the price.

"You can't have a Walmart product that you're trying to say is Nordstrom's," Schiro explained. "I absolutely believe that value is not about having the lowest price."

One way to spot a company that could have legal challenges is to assess whether the company's products are enough of a value that customers who are not part of the compensation plan are willing to purchase and repurchase the products at the company's current asking price. If you don't think they will, give the company a hard pass.

Several years ago, I was approached with the opportunity to acquire one of these companies. The private equity firm that owned the company had bought it at the height of the greed-inspired growth. Since that peak, the company's sales had fallen from more than $700 million to approximately $150 million. This PE firm had had enough and wanted to take advantage of a great year of performance and dump the investment. With more than $150 million in annual sales still being produced, we had the opportunity to purchase the company for less than $5 million in cash and a commitment to provide working capital. Knowing what I knew, and understanding the dynamics at play in the company, we turned down the opportunity. It sold two days later for three times that amount to a firm who could eliminate the management and overhead and profit from whatever reorder would remain.

Recently I had the opportunity to interview an executive who was a member of that company's finance department and I asked him what happened. He said that investors failed to ask simple questions about the value of the product.

"Their product was decent, but it was an overpriced product," he said. "I mean, they were selling monthly supplies of this stuff for one hundred thirty dollars a month for four bottles of this juice that really didn't have a lot of value. There was no real patent protection. There was no real substance behind the product. The company grew off of the opportunity message one hundred percent."

The failure of this company says nothing about the opportunity to find and harvest great investments in the channel, but rather shows the ignorance of the private equity investors who did this deal. They ignored the principles of identifying and rewarding value because they assumed there was something unique in direct selling that justified the abandonment of reason.

In my interview with LifeVantage CEO Darren Jensen, he emphasized how important product value is in building a lasting direct selling company.

"You truly have to have good products that are priced appropriately," Jensen said, "that are in high demand, and that are unique. I mean, that are *excellent*. And then the distributor experience has to be just incredible."

Sellers Who Add Value

In Don Miller's book *Building a Story Brand*, he introduces the concept that customers don't want to buy a company or product that displaces them as the hero. They want to remain the hero and hire someone or something that will be their "first mate" on their journey.

"The fatal mistake some brands make, especially young brands who believe they need to prove themselves, is they position themselves as the hero in the story instead of the guide," Don writes. "A brand that positions itself as the hero is destined to lose … Customers aren't looking for another hero; they're looking for a guide."[28]

Great direct sellers position their company's sellers as guides that help the customer's win. Origami Owl calls their distributors "designers" who help women create the perfect keepsake with their lockets. Beachbody's "coaches" are there to help hold customers accountable to their weight loss goals, and Rodan+Fields has "consultants" to help customers find the perfect skin care products.

Successful direct selling companies that have a clear value associated with having distributors as part of the channel are in stark contrast to others who have given little thought to their distributors' role in creating customer value. Several companies focus most of their time and incentives on the distributors only, and a few of these companies have allowed their top leaders to become the heroes. Initially, these companies and their top leaders wanted to emphasize the lifestyle possible for those who work hard and find success, but in time the sales organizations

---

[28] Miller, Don. *Building A StoryBrand: Clarifying Your Message So Customers Will Listen.* New York: HarperCollins Leadership, 2017.

confuse the purpose of the attention given to top leaders and turn their focus away from customers to these top leaders. Too often, top leaders (and many founders) believe their own press clippings and become self-appointed icons who lose touch with their customers and the needs of new distributors.

In the past, Amway and the companies that followed after would tell prospects about the "waste" that existed in the distribution channel as the product made its way from manufacturer to brick-and-mortar retailers. They would then explain that the company was taking the money paid to advertising and distribution middle men and rerouting it to Amway distributors who would do both the marketing and take on the duty of supplying products to their friends and neighbors (this is where the term "distributor" originated to describe those who sell, and though not as accurate anymore, it's a term that continues to be used). At that point in history the message made sense and seemed to leave room in the economics for direct selling distributors.

But customers and channels have changed. Today's customers have become more comfortable purchasing from outside the retail box and have become more sensitive to add-on expenses in the distribution channel. Today, the push to drive direct-to-consumer online sales provides plenty of "bypass the middleman" buying opportunities. Amway's old argument for the value of their distributors is no longer valid.

The challenge for direct selling companies is to replace that story with a reasonable argument for the value added by their "consultants" or "coaches" or "designers." Too often companies fail to define a role for their distributors and give no thought to articulating their value. Customers then conclude that the distributor's purpose is self-serving—that they are just an unnecessary cost. No customer wants to think that they are needlessly paying to enrich someone who does not add value to their experience.

Companies that don't provide a role and a reason for using distributors as value-added members of the channel must differentiate their products to clearly justify their price point, or they face failure. These companies don't experience immediate failure, but certain failure. Many of these companies may actually have impressive growth. Some may see such significant sales growth that professional investors are willing to abandon their own judgment of value with the argument that just because they don't understand why someone would pay that much for this special berry juice doesn't mean others don't value the product at that price point.

How do companies that lack consumer value and a purposeful role for distributors grow in the short term? Their growth is fueled by greed. The compensation plan used by these companies is designed to enrich distributors and it works perfectly as long as they can find enough distributors who meet minimum purchase requirements. If the company is good at telling the success stories of their early distributors and showing the money being made by these few, the greed-inspired growth continues. Eventually, the company can't lay track fast enough to keep that train moving and the growth not only slows, but the company experiences a spiraling death because the product doesn't have sufficient consumer benefit to keep people engaged if they are not making money.

Whether one is looking at the product or the persons inserted into the channel to deliver the product, every aspect of the company's offer must be delivering value. Even when there is great value, the company has to figure out how to message it and incentivize distributors for consistently preforming the behaviors that will capture that value.

In direct selling, as in all other methods of taking a product to market, companies need to be purposeful in assigning a value-adding role to every channel partner. Distributors shouldn't be allowed to play the role of heroes—even if it helps recruit other distributors in the short term, and they shouldn't be allowed to be seen as self-serving. Customers must be able to readily identify that the distributors add value in their transaction, not simply add an unnecessary expense.

Shared Via a Simple Sales System

The previous discussion about the importance of personal development notwithstanding, great direct sellers simplify the selling so little training is required. Several years ago, Success Partners, the publisher of *Success Magazine* and *Direct Selling News*, published a channel primer that stated, "No direct sales company had reached sales of $10 million or more a month with a focus on more than one product or service." Whether or not that claim can be proven, the principle is directionally accurate. Direct sellers are at best part time representatives who need a very simple system for engaging new customers and/or new distributors.

I asked Paul Adams, a leading consultant to direct sellers and a principal involved in the research done by Success Partners, if he felt that statement was still true today. Adams said that it was true, but with one caveat.

"I think it is the focus on the lead story," he said. "Every company has multiple products, but success boils down to understanding the lead product story that is going to get somebody interested and then keeping an extreme focus on that product story. Simplicity is the difference maker."

In my experience, simplicity involves both a focus on a single product, ingredient or system and a methodology of engaging with prospects that leaves even the newest of distributors thinking, "I can do that!"

Single Focus "On-Ramps"

One example of a simple system was the brilliant social media program created by Younique in the company's early days. They created a simple mobile phone application that allowed distributors to take photos of their face showing one side with their mascara and the other without. Younique salespersons (mostly women) would publish these photos on their social media accounts and would get immediate responses from friends and family wanting to learn more. A few years into the company's success, I had the chance to tour Younique's office and distribution center and to interview their CEO and co-founder, Derek Maxfield. When I walked into their small lobby, I was struck by the number of products on display. I had assumed Younique had only their famous mascara. In my interview with Maxfield that day, I asked how much of their sales came from their mascara product versus the other few dozen products they had in their line.

"Our mascara makes up fifty percent of our sales, and the other fifty percent of sales comes as a result of our mascara," Derek replied.

In other words, they had made it easy to drive interest using one highly visual product, built a methodology of using that product to introduce new customers to the company, and then became very good at selling other products to customers during and after their order of mascara.

At Beachbody, we had reasonable success when our sales agents, called "coaches," attempted to sell the company's fitness products or its flagship nutrition drink "Shakeology." However, the company's real growth came when we introduced the "Beachbody Challenge." To support the Beachbody Challenge, we simplified the product into a "Challenge Pack" and created a methodology of attracting new customers using a weight-loss challenge.

Coaches were encouraged to start challenge groups every few weeks and to invite those interested in losing weight and getting in better shape to join their FREE groups. They then recommended that all group participants start with a Challenge Pack. That simple system made it easy for new distributors to talk about our products. It gave them language to use to engage customers, was designed around social media and encouraged a frequency of engaging new customers that raised the bar on productivity. In short, every new coach would learn of our system of selling and would say, "I can do that!" and they did.

This new system was understood by coaches and became an engine of growth because it required almost no training. Coaches had a "copy and paste" system to follow to achieve sales. Recruiting new coaches was also simple. Coaches were taught to simply listen for customers who talked about being asked if they lost weight and were given language to turn those conversations into recruiting opportunities with the simple question, "Have you ever thought of doing what I do?"

After the introduction of the Beachbody Challenge, growth accelerated at a three-year compound annual growth rate (CAGR) above 70% and a five-year CAGR of more than 50%.

Systems Drive Marketing and Operational Efficiencies

With a simple sales system in place, Beachbody began to align its marketing, new product cadence, and sales incentives. The company introduced a monthly and annual sales incentive that rewarded success in working that system and avoided wasted spend on marketing programs and sales promotions that did not work. New products were introduced at predictable intervals that supported both seasonal interest in weight loss and the natural timing built into the selling system. New fitness programs were launched as part of a Challenge Pack bundle that included the same component parts (avoiding new training) and priced at one of three predictable price-points, all delivering great value to customers and a strong retail commission for the selling coach.

Every Success has a System

Every successful direct selling company has a simple sales system, but surprisingly few company executives understand what their company's system is. That is a bold claim, but years of experience have confirmed it in company after company. How can a company have success and not understand the system that is generating their sales? Often the system driving sales is discovered by the independent sales field leaders. Their experience, trial and error, and everyday connection with customers provides them the perfect opportunity to create, refine and perfect a system of sales. Shockingly few companies have taken the time to learn exactly what method and tactics their field leaders are using to generate sales. For many, (perhaps most), the independent field leaders define the system and teach their teams with little or no support from the company.

Often senior marketing executives have no real field experience and while they understand much about direct selling, they have never taken the time to understand the compensation system. I can make this claim because I started my career as the senior marketing executive at USANA Health Sciences and tried to get by without understanding the compensation plan for many months. Fearing that field leaders would be shocked to learn of my ignorance in something so important to them, I avoided deep dive learning sessions with successful field leaders and didn't realize I was not only ignorant when it came to understanding how distributors were paid, but I was also flying blind without an understanding of how our products were actually being sold to customers and how new distributors were being recruited. I've since learned that I was not alone. Many executives continue to have the same experience.

It wasn't until my experience at Beachbody that I came to understand the cost of my ignorance. When company executives don't truly understand the field's tactics and needs, they waste much of their marketing budget creating tools that never get used or even worse, new products that actually work against the selling system (more about that later). In fact, the tools often confuse new distributors who are being taught how to sell using one system and then are given tools by the company that clearly would be used to support another way of selling. The result: these new distributors often do nothing, and growth slows.

Misfit sales tools created by a company ignorant of its field's selling system also serve to divide corporate executives from field leaders. Why? Field leaders who want to be seen as being loyal put on a grateful face when tools are introduced and then out of fear of being labeled as a rebel, they hide their training and system even further from the company executives, thus perpetuating the cycle of misunderstanding.

One example of a company who didn't initially understand the selling system developed in the field is Herbalife at the beginning of one of their multiple waves of success. One of the company's waves of success in the United States came as a result of a program developed in Mexico. Rather than attempt to sell a monthly supply of their leading product Formula 1®, Herbalife's distributors in Mexico offered single servings from their home or workplace and called them "nutrition clubs." At first, Herbalife's executives reportedly didn't understand the program and even tried to prevent it from being taught in the U.S. despite the fact that it worked in the Latino communities. Fortunately for Herbalife, they were not successful in stopping this practice and eventually were forced to support it. Herbalife's impressive growth in the U.S. Latino community started as a result of this distributor-led sales system that was imported from Mexico by field leaders, and then eventually embraced by the corporate team.

In the spring of 2017, Nu Skin had a sudden and unexpected revival of sales in the United States. Despite the company's impressive investment in research and development and significant corporate efforts to increase sales, the new sales surge came from an almost forgotten product Nu Skin had been selling for more than ten years. Why? Led by the success of a new distributor in the United Kingdom and follow-on success by a new distributor in the U.S., Nu Skin's field leaders learned how to use social media to share before and after pictures of Nu Skin's AP 24® Whitening Fluoride Toothpaste to drive demand and increase sales. Then-outgoing CEO of Nu Skin, Truman Hunt, smiled as he told me that the toothpaste had been in their portfolio for years with few sales and no recent changes. One distributor took a decade-old product and turned it into a hit with a simple and powerfully effective system for selling via before and after pictures on social media.

Nu Skin executives were wise enough to set aside other initiatives and align behind the momentum of both the product and the social sharing method of selling. Newly appointed Nu Skin CEO Ritch Wood had a sexy, tech-focused strategy to talk about as he took over, and the company has followed its field to deploy tech tools designed to support the simple system. As is so often the case, Nu Skin's selling system was accidentally discovered by distributors with a combined tenure of fewer than six months with the company. To the credit of Nu Skin's management team, they were wise and humble enough to recognize and capitalize on the system and reap its benefits.

Few Executives Understand the Field's Sales System

Great selling systems are central to the success of direct selling companies, and yet because so few corporate executives have field experience the many not only don't know what system their field is using, they don't even understand a system should or does exist. Company after company has seen growth slow and spiral down because corporate executives made changes to their pricing, product offerings or messaging that inadvertently disrupted the selling system the field created. Even Beachbody saw its growth slow when the company's new digital platform was first introduced without proper consideration given to its impact on the economics and recurring revenue of Team Beachbody coaches.

Another good example is the rise and fall of skin care direct seller Arbonne. Arbonne experienced hockey stick growth (approximately $500 million in less than 3 years) as a result of their field's selling system. Field leaders taught their teams to drop off a full skin care system to prospects with this offer: "I want you to try this amazing product line, and I'm so confident you're going to love it that I'm going to allow you to try it for a week. If you love it, which I think you will, I'm going to stop by next week to pick up a check. If you don't like it, I'll pick up the product and you owe me nothing."

Arbonne's selling system worked and gave new customers and new distributors immediate confidence in the quality of the product. The company grew to more than $800 million in annual sales, but their private equity investors followed counsel they received from a consultant with little field experience and a conservative CFO, and decided the system was too risky. Investors demanded that the executive team stop the practice. The result was tragic, and the company began its free fall that didn't end until the company's sales had fallen to less than 50% of their peak. In 2009, the company reported sales of just $270 million. Only bankruptcy prevented Arbonne from being ruined by the misstep, but the private equity holders who had pushed for the change were forced to abandon their investment and leave it to debt holders who eventually salvaged a return nearly ten years later with the 2018 sale of the company to worldwide cosmetics and beauty brand Groupe Rocher.

While reasonable minds can disagree on the ethics or risk associated with the sales system employed by Arbonne's field, the critical learning is that Arbonne's board failed to properly understand and account for the essential role of the sales system. They did not understand that you cannot disrupt or stop a field from using a sales system unless you work with them to replace the system with something equally effective. Without exception, when a sales system is stopped and no thought is given to its replacement, the company's sales begin to decline rapidly.

New Products Must Fit the System

New products are often thought of as the key driver to increase growth. However, great direct selling companies understand the sales system being used by their distributors and make sure new products don't disrupt that system. Great companies work with field leaders to ensure that new products are introduced with an accompanying sales system, or deliberately teach distributors to continue to focus on the "lead story" and how to use the new product as a follow-on opportunity for existing customers or for prospects who don't respond to the lead.

For example, catalog companies like Avon, Home Interiors, Pampered Chef and Thirty-One Gifts rely on innovative seasonal products to give customers a reason to return to a party or look through their most recent catalog. Executives from these companies argue that managing the product pipeline is one of their most important responsibilities. However, companies that rely on a hero product and who have a field that understands how to use that hero product to acquire new customers and distributors will struggle to sell new products.

I learned this lesson early in my career at USANA Health Sciences, where we had a sales force that was leading with our core vitamin and mineral product called the Essentials. The company's founder was a scientist and the story told by our distributors all led to the Essentials. We became convinced that we needed a skin care line and launched a very good line with a tie-in to the company's science-based founding. The line initially sold out as current distributors and customers ordered the product to sample it for themselves and their family. To make sure we could keep up with demand, we acquired a manufacturer to make the product for us. But in the end, it never grew beyond the current base and never became a significant seller. In fact, the entire line made up less than ten percent of sales and the field struggled to find any new customers for any of our products until they decided to ignore the new skin care line and to go back to telling the story they knew about the Essentials.

A Model for Finding New Product Fit

Having experienced hockey stick growth and serious declines over the years, Nu Skin broke with the channel's long-standing tradition of introducing new products with a "surprise." During his tenure as CEO of Nu Skin, Truman Hunt threw out the long-standing practice of keeping all new products as closely guarded secrets. Nu Skin instead developed a thorough process of allowing qualifying leaders to respond to new product ideas years before they were to be launched. These leaders understood the field's selling systems and knew how to prepare for and adapt their systems to make the most of new products without disrupting those systems. In other words, the new product collaboration was not so much about whether or not the distributors liked the product, but more importantly included a dialogue about how they could sell the product given the current selling system they were using. To date, Nu Skin is one of the only companies that practices this collaborative method of including sales process in their new product development, and to their credit are one of the few companies that has seen incremental sales from new product introductions. The system they use today has been adapted over the years, but they have pioneered a process of collaboration that other companies would do well to learn from and employ.

As investors evaluate companies, looking for and understanding the system used to engage new customers and to begin a dialogue with prospective distributors is essential. Great board members ask management to explain how new products will support and not disrupt current selling systems and make sure management understands the selling systems that are driving or have driven growth.

The best companies work hand-in-hand with their field leaders to create a unified marketing and sharing system that makes it easy for the field and leaves new reps thinking "I can do that!" and leaves company management crystal clear in their understanding of how they can deploy company resources to support that system. Today, far too many companies leave the selling system to their independent distributors, and that's to everyone's detriment.

Stickiness

Great social sharing companies are sticky—customers and distributors find a reason that keeps them involved in the community and keeps them purchasing product. As in other industries, successful social sharing companies build value by acquiring and keeping customers, but that value grows exponentially when they are able to acquire and retain distributors or sellers at a similar rate.

Stickiness and retention can be measured using the same metrics, but they aren't the same thing. Retention is more transactional. Retention can be improved by instituting mechanisms like subscription or autoship orders and will be impacted by the type of product and the product's effectiveness. For example, companies that sell consumable products will naturally show a higher retention if they deliver on the product promise so that the consumer values and wants to reorder it. We will talk in more detail about retention and distinguish it from reactivation in Chapter 9, but for now, let's stay focused on stickiness.

Stickiness includes the mechanics and science of retention, but it also includes intangibles or the cultural attributes of a company and its leaders. Stickiness is a measure of loyalty and commitment and is the hard-to-measure feelings that cause a customer or distributor to remain part of the community in whatever role, despite setbacks and failures. Stickiness is what allowed USANA Health Sciences and Herbalife to weather ugly public criticism attacks and continue to grow.

More than most channels of distribution, social selling companies need stickiness. Distributors are only paid when they sell something. Most have no previous selling experience and probably would say they "don't like to sell." Stickiness is what helps a distributor ignore the friends and family members who encourage them not to join that "pyramid thing." Stickiness keeps a seller sharing despite hearing 'No!" more often than "Yes!" Great social sharing companies have stickiness, but not all stickiness is created equal because not all sources of stickiness can be controlled and counted on to continue to generate long-term enterprise value.

Stickiness and Enterprise Value

In direct selling, stickiness can be a result of something the company is doing right (deliberately or by accident), or in some cases might be due to the loyalty a customer feels to a distributor or corporate leader. In some rare incidences, a direct selling company can have little or no enterprise value because all of the stickiness is attached to things the company can't control. Not all stickiness is of equal value, and it's critical to understand who or what the company's customers and/or distributors are loyal to:

The Product. The best scenario is that the company's loyalty is centered in the product and its benefits. As long as the enthusiasm is based on real, defendable benefits, product loyalty is a great sign that there is enterprise value. For more than a decade, AdvoCare maintained more than $100 million in revenue (some years higher, some years lower) primarily because of the stickiness of their hero product "Spark." Despite poor flavors, a constant flow of different corporate leadership and other challenges, customers and distributors felt such a difference in their energy levels that they "had to have their Spark." A product like Spark with a strong and loyal user base is evidence of enduring enterprise value.

The Company Culture. Many direct sellers will talk about their loyalty to a company in terms of the social, emotional or personal development benefits they receive because of their involvement with it. While these benefits alone would not sustain a company, company culture can create enterprise value and is one of the most difficult benefits for competitors to copy. Company culture is defined as "the way we do things," and most great direct selling companies have a way of doing things that employees and field participants identify as unique and different.

Mary Kay Cosmetics is a company whose founder was the driving influence until her death, and then the company "institutionalized" the Mary Kay way of doing business. Some companies build their culture around the way they care for customers. Some build it around the attention they give to product quality. A few have become an extension of religious movements. But most start with rules and values and a way of doing things as espoused by the founder.

Several direct selling companies were started by founders who wanted the company to reflect their religious values and beliefs. Thirty-One and Noonday Collections both are open about the fact that their names were inspired by Biblical verses. However, having a founder and culture that is guided by religious values is different than companies and founders who have positioned themselves as a religious movement.

A few companies have assumed an evangelical culture and some leaders see the company as an extension of "God's work on the earth."

There is more than one company that actually holds religious services as part of their company meetings. I have become aware of more than one company with top leaders who have evangelized other participants, held baptisms during company events—at least one in the lobby fountain of a large five-star hotel. Years ago, one now public direct selling company endured (with significant loss in sales) a multi-year power struggle when board members tried to replace the company's openly evangelical CEO with a "professional executive." After more than one proxy fight, a short re-emergence of that CEO for a time, and significant management turnover, the company has become less open in their evangelism.

No matter your personal beliefs, it is important to be able to identify if the culture of the company is influenced by or in fact an outreach of a religious worldview so that you are able to understand the culture that participants are sticking to.

Founder's Charisma. Almost all direct selling companies have a charismatic founder at their head. Great founders understand the importance of culture and carefully curate the company's culture in all of their communications and events from day one.

When I became the CEO of Origami Owl, the company had seen some retraction from their peak sales. Some of the debt holders had recommended that the company hire an interim CEO (my predecessor) who was suggesting that it was time to move on from the founders. After spending a week on the road observing company meetings and another week talking with field leaders, my advice was the complete opposite: we needed to center the company again on the founders vision and the culture they had created. That became my mission, and when it was accomplished, I stepped aside as CEO.

In the case of Origami Owl, the stickiness of the company came from the desire distributors had to be part of the enthusiasm and excitement that emanated from the founders Chrissy and Bella Weems, Tyson Basha and Shawn Maxwell. Their unorthodox, "throw caution to the wind" approach to business and life created a movement that others wanted to join. Before "professional management" was brought in, the distributors had been willing to stick around despite product defects, periods of out of stock and other challenges. Distributors stayed because they loved the experiences the founders created and the way the founders made them feel when they were in their presence or on a call with them.

Founder-driven culture, like that at Origami Owl, can be powerful and valuable. However, some founders have a way of making it all about themselves and can inspire a cult-like loyalty to them personally. When founders become intoxicated by the attention they get from the field, they can often let their egos put them at odds with other corporate shareholders and sometimes can unknowingly erode the field's loyalty.

While investors often underestimate the loyalty the field feels for a company founder or top corporate executive, often founders and top executives overestimate the field's loyalty to them. Early in my career, the company I worked for flew its top field leaders to a resort to announce a major change in pricing and compensation. The night before our meeting in a conference room at this resort, the management team gathered and the top sales VP (who had recruited the top income earners years ago when the company was founded) announced that he would not go on stage and make these major announcements unless he was first made CEO of the company. The company did need a new CEO, but he wasn't it. After a long night of negotiation with the founder, the sales VP did agree to go on stage and make the announcement, and two months later the unthinkable happened—he was fired. That sales leader went on to start a company that did well. He even took a few field leaders with him, but nothing he created has succeeded like the company he left, and no one studying the financials of that company could identify the date that the "too important to let go" sales VP was fired.

USANA, Mary Kay, Herbalife and other large public companies have survived the departure of a charismatic founder or early corporate sales leader, but not without a period of painful withdrawal. Investors with a relatively short-term time horizon (three to seven years) should take care to understand the motives, ethics, and ability of the founders and proceed with caution if they believe a change will occur for any reason after their investment in the company. Loyalty to a founder or senior executive can contribute to enterprise value only if the founder or executive is aligned with and committed to shareholder value and the same time horizon.

Field Leader's Loyalty. With direct sellers, it is imperative to distinguish the source of the culture because it could be company sponsored or it could be inspired by and created within a field sales organization. If the cultural benefits are delivered by independent distributors who could leave and take their culture with them, investors need to understand that flight risk and become comfortable in the loyalty of that field leader and the company's ability to retain him or her.

While I was leading Beachbody's social selling division, I became acquainted with a field leader who had been successful in earning $20K or more a month in several companies. Her success was driven by her uncanny marketing and communication skills and she had used those skills to build a large and loyal organization that would in fact follow her wherever she went. At the time we talked, she guaranteed that she could generate millions of dollars of new sales if I worked with her. However, these sales would come from a pre-existing sales team that was loyal to her and followed her from company to company and sometimes participated as sales reps for more than one company at a time. In fact, she told me that her organization was at that time already involved in more than one direct selling business. While this lack of loyalty is rare in the U.S., I'm told it is more common in Asia. We chose not to do business with her and opted instead to continue to build with coaches whose product success had created high loyalty to our brand and product offering.

Most top field leaders believe that their sales organization is loyal to them. Most believe that if they leave, their entire team will follow them to other companies. Only rarely is that true. Time and again, top leaders get offended and leave a company or ignore company rules and are terminated only to find that they have little if any influence on motivating their organization to leave. But remember that I said "most." There are instances when leaders can and will take their business and go elsewhere, and I have seen that happen and watched companies lose hundreds of millions of dollars in sales as a result.

Signs Loyalty May Be Low

Company owners should be concerned about losing top leaders if any or all of these variables are true:

Sales are Concentrated. In a few rare circumstances, a sales leader has brought corporate customers or international field groups to a direct selling company that represented significant amount of sales. For example, a large corporation that offers a pre-paid legal service to its employees might have a single distributor who owns the relationship with a key client. In the past, B2B direct sellers with new owners were cavalier about the role of their direct sellers and assumed that the company—not the sales representative—owned the customer relationship. Buyer beware as these same companies have watched hundreds of millions of dollars of revenue walk to a competitor with the sales representative, who in the end owned the relationship.

Sales Leaders Were Acquired with Their Team. A few companies have engaged in the controversial activity of recruiting sales leaders from one company to come to theirs. If there are companies that have had long-term success with this practice, they have not been public about it. There are plenty of examples of companies that have experienced a short-term burst of sales only to see sales decline as those they recruit move on to other opportunities.

The danger in this practice is in the fact that it exposes a company to professional networkers, a group of gypsy-like distributors with loyalty only to their earning potential. These groups have worked together in the past and have made a career of moving from one company to the next to exploit opportunities. These groups exist in the United States but are prevalent in parts of Asia, particularly Korea. Sometimes they see a company with a rich compensation plan that hasn't been thoroughly vetted when it comes to the rules and payouts, and they see a way to earn lots of income with very little sales or by manipulating the compensation plan in a way the designers of the plan had failed to anticipate. Others sign agreements with companies that require little or no actual results and after exhausting the cash from their agreement, they move on to the next opportunity.

However, the professional networkers come, it is important to understand that they are also highly likely to go, and if they have brought a team of distributors with them, they are also likely to take them when they move on. Beware of companies that grow in chunks or brag about attracting top leaders and organizations from other companies. Many of the spectacular failures in direct selling told similar stories during their glory days.

Corporate Executives Aren't Trusted by the Field. If top field leaders leave, and the remaining leaders have little to no relationship of trust with the company's executive team, it can lead to wholesale losses in field leaders. On occasion, direct selling companies grow despite executives who don't know their sales force and don't understand their business. Rarely is this the case when a founder is still in place, but sometimes the founder has passed, leaving the company to family. In other cases, the company's founder was replaced under pressure from investors or lenders.

One large direct seller had grown to nearly one billion dollars in annual sales. Most of the sales had come under the direction of a dynamic corporate leader. When that leader's relationship with the owners turned sideways and the leader was replaced, the company began a multi-year decline and lost hundreds of millions in sales. Their sales dropped not because their executives didn't know their business or even have relationships with field leaders, but because the field leaders didn't trust the capability of the remaining corporate team. Top leaders received mixed messages from the corporate team still in place. Their lack of confidence left them unable to recruit and motivate others. Eventually, both field and corporate leaders were left chasing a downward spiraling company.

Understanding where the field's loyalty lies is a critical component of being able to preserve and grow enterprise value. Loyalties can be properly aligned, but only when there is a plan in place that accurately accounts for the current loyalties. Investing in a company with a customer or sales base that is loyal to variables you don't own or can't control is a sure way to lose your capital.

Now that you understand the Five S's that make up best practices for companies in the channel, it's time to turn our attention to due diligence. In the chapters that follow I will outline suggestions for due diligence specific to direct selling and detail the questions you should ask to make sure you avoid making a poor investment.

Chapter 5

Due Diligence: The Company and Management

All of the insight offered to this point has provided you the background you need to separate the potentially great companies from the pretenders. Now it is time to pull together a summary of the research I recommend to anyone looking to invest time or money in a direct selling company. This is the first of three chapters on due diligence, and at the end of Chapter 7 I include the top ten due diligence items all in a single, simple document to help you make "go" or "no go" investment decisions.

The diligence items listed below pre-suppose that you have completed the general financial and background due diligence you would do on any company in any industry. In this chapter and the two that follow, I've outlined the channel-specific issues that most often lead to significant erosion of sales and/or enterprise value. We will begin with specific issues you should look for as you evaluate the management team and their business practices. We will then suggest ways for you to better understand the strength of the independent sales team, and finally we'll identify key performance indicators and some channel-specific financial analysis you'll want to complete before you make an investment decision.

The Founder

A few months after I joined the Beachbody Board of Directors, one of the partners of LNK invited me to their office where I asked him about their decision to invest in Beachbody. In the interview, I learned that the company prioritized management over most other variables, and in the case of Beachbody, the founder Carl Daikeler was someone LNK had confidence in after their first meeting. It is safe to say that without Carl, LNK would likely not have invested. I suspect that most investors look closely at the management team, but in direct selling, most investors would be wise to follow LNK's example and give careful consideration to the founder – especially if the founder continues to be the primary operator.

Most of the younger (<15 years in business) direct selling companies have a founder or founders who still play an essential role. While it is not unique for companies of that age to have active founders, what can be unique in direct selling is the influence the founder has on the company—especially on the independent sales force. Many founders of direct selling companies have personally recruited family and friends to be the founding distributors. During the early years of a company, the relationship between most founders and their top sellers becomes very, very close. By the time a company has had some success, often it is difficult for employees and distributors to separate the values of the company from the values of the founder.

Given the characteristically deep relationship between founders and their field, investors need to take account of the founder and make sure her/his goals align with their plans for the company. Do the founder's values and business practices match the values and practices you believe are important? Does s/he have the necessary skills to continue in a meaningful role with the company? Is the founder's timeline aligned with the investors? David Stirling is the CEO of natural oils giant doTERRA, and he warns investors to be wary of the motives of a founder seeking capital.

"Direct selling companies rely heavily on relationships," Stirling said, "and founders looking to 'cash out' might not have the level of continual commitment to keep the company strong."

Investors should assume that the founder will continue to be critical to the company's future and should consider the founder's interest in continuing in the company and their ability to provide value beyond that of chief relationship officer. Here are some considerations in evaluating founders:

Founders as Operators

Most founders have assumed the role of President and CEO even when they have little previous management experience and often without any previous business experience. Sometimes Founder/CEOs can be more than a little bit of a challenge to manage because they often are treated as just a little lower than deity by their field and employees. A few of these founders have come to believe that they are great executives when those who report to them would argue otherwise.

It is not enough to understand the potential weakness of a founder and to expect that you will be able to overcome those weaknesses by surrounding the founder with disciplined operators. You must be sure the founder is, in fact, self-aware of weaknesses and willing to fully embrace the discipline you anticipate. For example, one of the channel's only serial entrepreneurs (who we will call David) has inspired independent sales agents and built at least two companies with sales of more than $100 million. However, investors who have worked with this executive and three-time founder have described him using this analogy:

"David is the most successful motivator I have ever worked with, but he doesn't have a single operating bone in his body. He could convince tens of thousands of people to join him to dig a hole to the center of the earth, and after everyone has gathered, he would turn to those around him and ask, 'Did anyone bring a shovel?'"

David built a company that attracted hundreds of millions of investor dollars, but almost immediately after the money was received the investors realized they couldn't control the decisions made by David. One former executive recounted that the investors brought in a COO, then a CFO and required that all expenditures be approved. Both the CFO and COO were very strong leaders. Both executives understood the channel. Neither were entirely successful in bringing discipline to the CEO or the company, but instead created an awkward rift that everyone could witness. David eventually moved out of the office and tried to run sales from his vacation home in a different state. In the end, the company failed entirely, but not until after years of significant investor involvement, a bankruptcy that gave investors authority to remove the founder and CEO, and eventually a fire sale of all the company's assets.

Former Distributors as Founders

Many of today's companies are founded by CEOs who were successful distributors but who have never had operating experience. One such founder told me, "I had no idea what it took to run a company. This is so much more difficult than what I did as a field leader."

One of the channel's leading marketing consultants, Paul Adams, said that in his experience many of the companies who fail are run by founders who aren't willing to admit that they don't know enough and need help. Paul said, "I can point to plenty of companies through the years that were run with an arrogance that comes with the success of being a good field leader. You know the type: 'I made a lot of money as a distributor and now I'm going to start my own company. I know all there is to know.' Those are the ones that tend to come and go."

Field experience is helpful but is not broad enough to prepare a founder to be a great CEO. Founders with success as distributors should also show that they have been willing to go out and find equally experienced management to lead the operational and technical functions.

Founder Ethics

In Chapter 4 we talked about the role the company's founder plays in establishing the culture of the company and how some founders view the company as an extension of a religious movement. The founder's impact on culture and company values is enormous and founders create deep-seated habits that are often hard to correct. However, in a channel that naturally attracts skepticism, *it is critical that the founder has ethics beyond reproach.* Most of the time, companies that attract regulatory scrutiny do so because the company's founder is unknowingly caught on record encouraging field leaders to do or say things that are illegal, immoral, or just plain wrong. If you have any doubts about the founder's commitment to building a company the right way, don't risk your reputation by partnering with him/her.

Due Diligence Tip #1: FOUNDER ALIGNMENT

Don't do a deal with a founder you don't trust and who doesn't have the self-awareness to accept the professional help you expect to provide.

Management Team

After more than a dozen years in investment banking, Eric Roth became a partner at MidOcean Private Equity. I asked Eric what surprised him the most after making the move to a PE firm and he said it was the amount of time they spend focusing on senior management and executive leadership.

"It's not number one," he said. "It's like number one, two, three and four."

In my experience, direct selling companies don't usually put that kind of rigor into the development of their management team, so it is often the first consideration when professional investors become involved. In assessing the management team of a direct selling company and making decisions on future executives, there are a few channel-specific considerations:

Attitude Toward Direct Selling

All members of the management team should have a favorable disposition to the version of direct selling practiced by the company. Too often, executives and board members have joined the company with the hope that they could convince the owners to abandon direct selling. Even a small antagonism for the channel eventually leads to an intolerable working relationship and necessitates an expensive replacement.

On more than one occasion, I have worked with executives and/or board members who don't like the channel and would prefer not to be doing business as a direct seller. These individuals are often hired with the hope that they will "come around," or their antagonism is ignored because of their functional expertise. In my experience, these hires never work. Their bias always expresses itself and leads to a lack of unity with other members of the executive team. In every case, these antagonists find a way to exit the business as soon as an opportunity presents itself.

Direct Selling Experience

While functional executives (finance, operations, IT, etc.) must have a favorable attitude toward direct selling, they do not need direct selling experience. Functional expertise is all that is required of most executives and I believe it is helpful to have at least one or two members of a management team who bring insight and experience from outside the channel.

Direct selling should be a requirement of the entire sales leadership team and at least one director or above with direct selling experience should be in place in marketing, IT and legal/compliance. Eventually, any willing executive can learn to understand the space, but the subtlety of the nuances in the channel make the learning curve long to navigate, and lessons can come at a high cost to the business.

Many of the CEOs I've spoken with talked about the importance of making sure executives (and board members) who are new to the channel get some formal training. Bouncer Schiro, the CEO of Stream Energy emphasized, "I would explain the comp plan ad nauseam to new board members and or new executives." Having made the mistake of trying to be a senior executive without a knowledge of the company's compensation plan, I would strongly echo Schiro's advice. I will talk more about how to train new boards and advisors in Chapter 11.

Loyalty and Alignment to the Enterprise

Senior executives in this channel often develop a close relationship with field leaders and receive rock star treatment as they travel and relate with independent distributors. Too often, these executives learn to manipulate their field relationships to gain power and authority within the organization. This real or perceived power also shifts the executive's loyalty from the company and/or its owners to the field. The conflicting loyalty is manifest in leaking confidential information to the field leaders, fighting for events, programs or resources that benefit their favorite field leaders, and often in attempting to organize leaders in ways to benefit the executive and his/her interests in the company.

For example, in one direct selling company, a senior sales executive who had recruited many of the top distributors disagreed with the rest of the management team on a strategic change. This sales executive tried to convince the management team to NOT make the change planned. When he lost that argument, he used a whisper campaign to discredit members of the executive team and the planned change. Fortunately, the founder and the management team worked closely together to control information and were eventually able to implement a slow and deliberate plan to replace the senior sales executive.

Other companies have had a less favorable result. In one case, a CEO with channel-leading results was ousted by subordinates who played their field relationships and internal politics to yield power. That company experienced a sales drop of nearly half a billion dollars. More than one company has seen members of the senior team leave to start competing companies, recruiting employees and distributors to follow them.

Replacing Management

If you find an issue with the management team, it is important to understand that sometimes it can be more difficult to replace management in a direct selling company than it is in most privately held companies. That doesn't mean you shouldn't improve the management team. It just means you should be thoughtful about how you go about making the change.

"Outside investors probably don't appreciate how difficult it is in this industry to remove management because of the personal relationships that exist with the field," said Travis Ogden, CEO of Isagenix. "While it's a valid question and something that a board should debate if companies have declined, clearly, they should be looking at management, but I would just caution any investor to really take a hard look at whether it's necessary to make a change or not. Sometimes it might be necessary, but if it is, you have to be really careful. This is an attitude business and you don't want to spook the field. You don't want the field to think that senior management is abandoning ship for whatever reason. It's a sign of trouble, particularly if it's a field-facing executive. It's really hard to remove them. Make sure it really is necessary and they do it strategically and make sure you have a good story or reason for the field."

Due Diligence Tip #2: ALIGN MANAGEMENT

Don't settle for poor management, and make sure the team has the necessary channel attitude and experience, a positive attitude toward direct selling, and is aligned in creating enterprise value.

Regulatory Risk

In the past decade, a few public companies (Herbalife, Nu Skin, and USANA) have had activists attack their company and make public attempts to discredit their business model. While each of these attacks ended as spectacular failures, much of the misinformation they published lingers among investors. Many investors worry that direct selling companies could be suddenly put out of business by regulators, that they are in fact a pyramid scheme, or that there are other unknown regulatory factors that increase the risk of an investment in this channel. I will provide guidance that will help you understand the truth and avoid undue regulatory risk, but in the end, it's important that you obtain your own legal counsel from an experienced direct selling attorney to ensure that the company you are investing in is complying with channel best practices. In particular, you will want to have an experienced direct selling attorney review the company's commission plan.

Direct selling companies are regulated primarily by three government agencies. The consumer protection division of the state attorney general's office (State AG), the Federal Trade Commission (FTC), and, for companies with personal care products, the U.S. Food and Drug Administration (FDA). The State AG offices and FTC are primarily concerned about the financial claims and business opportunity claims made by a company while the FDA is looking at product claims. Remember, illegal claims can be made either by the company or by one of their independent distributors.

To help you assess the regulatory risks associated with a particular company, you'll need answers to the following questions before investing any time or money:

- **Is it possible the company will be shut down by government regulators?**
- **Is the company a pyramid scheme?**
- **Does the company or its distributors make income claims?**

- **Does the company or its distributors make product claims that are either illegal or insufficiently validated?**
- **Is the company's international business lawfully established?**

Without getting into a deep legal conversation—remember, you must consult an attorney for legal advice—let's take a look at each of these critical concerns.

Is it possible the company will be shut down?

It is unlikely that a company you invest in will be suddenly shut down by a regulator (especially if you've given consideration to the content in this chapter). It is unlikely, but not impossible. There are a few companies that have been suddenly shut down, but rarely have those actions surprised anyone who knew of the company's practices.

Direct selling carries the same type of regulatory risk as a pharmaceutical or a financial services company. Just like in those industries, the vast majority of companies understand the rules. They design their business practices to operate within those rules, and therefore they have limited risk. We all know that there have been a few bad banks, some unscrupulous investment houses and a handful of fraudulent insurance agencies. Though few in number, these bad apples make the world take notice. Likewise, there have been a few bad direct sellers who were operating illegal pyramid schemes disguised as legitimate direct sellers. To my knowledge, there have been less than five who have received "cease and desist" or *ex parte* temporary restraining orders (TRO) by the FTC.

On August 21, 2015, I was the CEO of Origami Owl Family of Brands. I was at work in my office when I received an alarming text from a long-time friend, at the time an executive at a direct seller called Vemma. He said that armed federal agents, along with local law enforcement—ten or more in all—had just burst into their office and "taken control." My friend sent a series of sparse but shocking texts describing how agents had ordered every employee to step away from their computers and told them the firm would be operated under the authority of a receiver. The FTC press release about the event read in part: "the court halted the deceptive practices, froze the defendants' assets, and appointed a temporary receiver over the business pending a trial."[29]

In an article published in the June 2018 edition of *Social Selling News*, Lois Greisman, associate director for the Division of Marketing Practices for the FTC, was asked at what point the FTC makes the decision to use a TRO to shut down a company without prior warning. Greisman was reported to have said, "… when the FTC believes that the harm to consumers is severe and that the money and people would conveniently disappear if notice were to be given, which would prevent us from providing any restitution to consumers."[30]

In the case of Vemma, the court attempted to use a receiver to avoid closing the company and try and preserve value. Why such swift and severe action on Vemma? Perhaps it was because the founder had a previous history that the FTC described in their press release: "The

---

[29] https://www.ftc.gov/news-events/press-releases/2015/08/ftc-acts-halt-vemma-alleged-pyramid-scheme, accessed May 22, 2019.
[30] https://socialsellingnews.com/features/the-ftc-shifts-its-target/, accessed May 23, 2019.

defendants are Vemma Nutrition Company, Vemma International Holdings Inc., Tom Alkazin, and Benson K. Boreyko, who is under a 1999 court order after settling with the FTC for his involvement with New Vision International Inc., a multilevel marketing company that sold nutritional supplements." In other words, Vemma's CEO Boreyko had already agreed to a court order and the FTC concluded that he was ignoring that previous agreement.

The most public regulatory actions were against Herbalife, Amway (FTC) and Nu Skin (State AGs), and all of those actions ended with a fine, an agreement to change business practices or both. In fact, there are many executives who believe that because Congress has failed to provide clear statutory definitions to regulate the channel, most large direct sellers have publicly or privately had the FTC review their practices and some have reportedly entered into their own agreements with the FTC and continued with some modifications in their business practices. In my opinion, most companies that emerge from an FTC investigation are arguably better off and stronger.

Since I began writing this book, AdvoCare International announced that they would change their sales model from multi-level marketing to single-level marketing after confidential talks with the FTC. Here are the first two paragraphs from the company's announcement:

PLANO, Texas (May 17, 2019)—Today, AdvoCare International announces a revision of its business model from multi-level marketing to a direct-to-consumer and single-level marketing compensation plan. AdvoCare has been in confidential talks with the Federal Trade Commission about the AdvoCare business model and how AdvoCare compensates its Distributors. The planned change will impact Distributors who have participated in the multi-level aspect of the business. Those who currently sell only to customers will not be impacted and there will be no impact on Preferred Customers or retail customers' ability to purchase products.

"Over the years, we have made many changes to the AdvoCare policies as the regulatory environment has shifted. Based on recent discussions, it became clear that this change is the only viable option," says Patrick Wright, AdvoCare's Chief Executive Officer... The company gave notice to its more than 100,000 Distributors on May 17 that, effective July 17, 2019, AdvoCare will revise the business model to a single-level distribution model, paying compensation based solely on sales to direct customers. The Retail and Preferred Customer programs will remain intact...

Having served as the CEO of AdvoCare, I can confirm that the company had talks with the FTC over several years and based on my knowledge of the content of those discussions more than a year ago, I am as shocked as anyone about the outcome. My surprise means that there is more I don't know than what I know.

AdvoCare chose to make these changes to their model without engaging the help of the DSA, so it is unclear if the decision is precedent setting or simply a business decision, the outcome of which is yet to be determined. On May 27, 2019, long-time channel lawyer Jeffrey A. Babener wrote an article on the announcement in the WORLD OF DIRECT

SELLING that is worth reading. In that article Babener expresses the questions raised by AdvoCare's announcement.

"Nothing about the announcement changes the existing legal standards for pyramid vs. legitimate direct selling," he wrote. "Those standards weave their way from the *Koscot* case through *Amway* through *BurnLounge*. And the acid test is: Are distributor payments and commissions driven by recruitment and qualification in the plan, on the one hand, or sales to ultimate users?"[31]

Is the company a pyramid scheme?

According to the FTC's website, "The most widely-cited description of an unlawful MLM structure appears in the FTC's Koscot decision, which observed that such enterprises are "characterized by the payment by participants of money to the company in return for which they receive (1) the right to sell a product and (2) the right to receive in return for recruiting other participants into the program rewards which are *unrelated to the sale of the product to ultimate users*." In re Koscot Interplanetary, Inc., 86 F.T.C. 1106, 1181 (1975) {Emphasis added}.[32]

Said another way, do company distributors get paid for selling products that others actually consume?

This is where the channel's evolution to better define the difference between a distributor and a customer is relevant (more on this in Chapter 9). The best way to understand if the company you're looking at will be

---

[31] https://www.worldofdirectselling.com/advocare-abandons-mlm/, accessed May 28, 2019.
[32] https://www.ftc.gov/tips-advice/business-center/guidance/business-guidance-concerning-multi-level-marketing, accessed May 28, 2019.

accused of being an illegal pyramid scheme is to verify that there is customer demand for the products or to simply ask yourself if you believe the company's product offers good consumer value.

In your due diligence, ask what percentage of the company's sales are made to customers versus distributors, and make sure the definition of a customer is anyone who does NOT have a contract to be a distributor and is NOT simply a distributor who has yet to have success as a distributor. Companies with a large number of customers purchasing are simple to defend.

For now, companies with most of their sales coming from the personal consumption of the product by distributors may also be able to avoid regulatory challenges IF you are convinced that their products as priced are providing value to the end consumer independent of any business value. Many industry experts will argue that regulators will soon require that all companies have at least 51% of all sales coming from customers – those not affiliated in any way with the company's compensation plan.

It is possible to invest in a company and help them make the transition to be a consumer first direct seller, but that transition is possible only if the company's products/services have stand-alone value. If a company is selling products at prices beyond a reasonable value, you should be concerned. Your concern should increase if your company is making a profit on the sale of training (live or in the form of books or media), enrollment fees or anything else other than their core products. The concern is magnified if the company is paying commissions on any business tools, starter kits or training; paying commissions on "new recruits"; or requiring large upfront purchases of any kind.

In the previous chapter, I outlined the arguments for and against the process of recruiting distributors from other companies. It is important to note in this section that the practice of guaranteeing payment to a distributor who agrees to join your company from another company is beginning to be labeled as "paying for recruits", which the FTC has defined as the primary practice that defines an illegal pyramid scheme. In the September 2018 issue of *Social Selling News,* Jane Fergason, partner at law firm Foley & Lardner LLP, was quoted as saying, "I think the practice raises issues with pyramid laws because a distributor is supposed to be paid commissions on sales. But if you are receiving a guaranteed payment from a company regardless of the sales you may be making, there is an argument to be made that the company is paying you just for bringing people in, which is recruiting."[33]

Does the company make income claims?

The third major point the FTC is concerned about has to deal with income claims. In today's regulatory environment, income claims or lifestyle stories that make implied income claims must be accompanied by a fact sheet showing income earned by all distributors. Regulators are concerned about practices of inferring that all or most distributors obtain a certain income or lifestyle when in fact the stories told may represent less than 1% of all distributors. Even photos and images of lavish lifestyles can be troublesome. In the June 2018 issue of *Social Selling News*, Ambit Energy, the $1.2 billion energy services company, reportedly made the

[33] https://socialsellingnews.com/features/the-double-edged-sword-of-raiding-and-cross-recruiting/#more-2096, accessed May 23, 2019.

decision to remove all lifestyle imagery from its marketing materials (*Social Selling News*, June 2018, page 7).

If the company you are investing in is growing because distributors are using income claims to generate excitement – even if they can document those earnings – I would beware and would avoid investing in the company.

The best companies in the channel are careful about what they say and print regarding their income opportunity and most have become transparent in disclosing details about how many people are earning how much. Below are links (current as of publication) to a few companies who have done a good job disclosing income and earnings of all their distributors:

- **Melaleuca:**
  https://www.melaleuca.com/Introduction/Content.aspx?Page=Income_Statistics

- **Nu Skin:**
  https://www.Nu
  Skin.com/content/dam/office/n_america/US/en/business_materials/distearnings.pdf

- **Beachbody:**
  https://images.beachbody.com/coach-office/downloads/statement_of_independent_coach_earnings_Canada.pdf

- **Herbalife:**
  https://ir.herbalife.com/static-files/2ff07056-59bf-4db9-bb7ecde4bca50b06

- **USANA Health Sciences:**

  https://www.usana.com/media/File/Downloads/NA/BusinessTools/
  US-AveIncome.pdf

Does the company make product claims?

Direct sellers who offer nutrition and personal care products are subject to regulatory oversight by the FDA and to the Direct Selling Association's Code of Ethics. Some companies will encourage or even publish product claims that lack the scientific hurdle or fail to meet regulatory requirements for such claims. More often, distributors who have results they attribute to the product will tell their stories which they assert are true. Unfortunately, when it comes to product claims, truth is defined not by a user's experience but by hurdles set by regulators and too often resolving the discrepancies requires more discipline than many early stage direct sellers have.

Product claims are not only an issue in the U.S. but are a global issue with serious consequences. For example, in early 2019, China's State Administration for Market Regulation (SAMR) and the Ministry of Commerce summoned all 91 direct selling companies with licenses to operate in China and warned them to clean up their product manufacturing and to stop their distributors from making unlawful claims.[34] This summons had the effect of rattling U.S. public markets, and several

---

[34] https://www.nutraingredients-asia.com/Article/2019/02/06/China-direct-selling-All-91-firms-summoned-to-regulator-meeting-amid-100-day-clampdown#

publicly traded direct sellers with significant business in China saw their stocks tumble.

If the company you are considering is experiencing growth because of the product stories of distributors, make sure your due diligence includes a deep dive into the legality of those claims.

Are international operations lawfully established?

While most companies go into international markets with the proper product or opportunity registrations, a few have decided to sidestep local laws. Most international markets have product registration laws, and a few (like Canada) have business opportunity or compensation plan regulations.

I conducted an interview with the president of a mid-market international direct selling company. He expressed surprise that lenders doing due diligence on his company had little interest in how the company had developed international sales. (He asked not to be identified due to his firm's ongoing discussions with lenders).

"There are so many companies that expand to international markets using an NFR [not for resale] model," he said. "They have a tremendous amount of business internationally, but they're not well established in any market. They don't know if their compensation plan is legal. They don't have the licensing setup. They don't have their product registered. So do a little more due diligence on the risk profile of the international business, because that business, if not done right, can dry up pretty fast. And I've seen it happen."

Your due diligence should include questions about how many international markets they are in and what regulatory approvals they have for those countries. You should also ask to see sales and a P&L for each market (far too many markets are not profitable). If most of a company's foreign markets are being serviced via an NFR model, you should slow down and take a deeper dive.

If you want to get a quick read on how seriously the company approaches its international expansion, one good question to ask is, "How fast can you enter a new market?" The right answer to that question is "about a year" or "ten months if we push it." Devin Thorpe cautioned, "I would say that if you have an extremely competent international expansion then it takes about a year. It doesn't matter how many engineers you put on it. The regulatory approvals take time. And if you push it, you run the risk of testing the Foreign Corrupt Practices Act."

Due Diligence Tip #3: REGULATORY RISK

Make sure the company's commissions only reward product sales, that the products are priced at a reasonable value, and that distributors are not relying on unsubstantiated product or income claims. If the company is doing business in international markets, make sure it has proper registrations as required by each country.

Sales System or Engine of Growth

In his book *The E-Myth Revisited*, author Michael E. Gerber makes an observation that was written as a warning to small business owners but could just as well be wise advice to potential direct selling investors. He wrote:

> *If your business depends on you, you don't own a business—you own a job. And it's the worst job in the world because you're working for a lunatic.*

In other words, if the company you are investing in relies on personalities and fails to have a defined system in place for acquiring customers, buyer beware.

Assuming you are looking to invest in a company that is growing, you will want to do enough research to understand the company's system of growth. As you dig into this, you are likely to find that the company's engine of growth falls into one of three categories:

Personality Driven

The company has a founder or top distributor who is the keystone. A majority of sales and recruiting has something to do with this person and his/her story. If the company has a personality that is so essential for its continued growth, you aren't buying a business … you are becoming an employer who is vulnerable to the health and happiness of one person.

Field-Based Selling System

More often than not, a direct selling company has a selling system (or a few systems) that are well understood by the field but not thoroughly understood by the company. Often the executives of these companies will talk about their "system" in broad terms like "we sell in-home via parties," or "we have a person-to-person system." A system is a clear methodology that a new distributor would follow to sell a product. A good system enables every aspect of the transaction, from starting a conversation about the product to curating the prospect's interest to asking for the purchase and eventually to inviting the customer to become a distributor. Many companies leave the development of the system to the field, and therefore the company might have a system, but management doesn't completely know what it is. Having a system that is not understood is not as bad as not having a system, especially if you help the company do the work to identify the system(s).

The problem with field-based systems is that the management team's ignorance can cause them to make changes that have disastrous results. I've personally witnessed two companies that have seen sales fall by hundreds of millions of dollars because the management made "simple tweaks" that destroyed the engine of growth the field had worked so hard to develop.

Corporate-Driven System

Ideally, the field and corporate management will both understand and be united around a system of growth. This unity prevents costly management mistakes and wasted marketing and sales programs. It also allows the business to withstand personnel changes, whether in management or in the field.

Be warned that sometimes there are corporate-driven systems that are not embraced by the field or are not sustainable. As we've discussed earlier, any direct selling company that requires ongoing investments in advertising, direct response or distributor acquisition does not have a direct selling engine of growth and is wasting money on either compensation to distributors or in advertising or promotion dollars. Traditional marketing spend can enhance the direct selling channel, but if those dollars are the primary method of customer or distributor acquisition, the company has a problem that is not simple to fix.

Having and thoroughly understanding the system of growth will ensure your investment dollars are likely to be deployed in ways that will increase enterprise value and improve results.

Due Diligence Tip #4: IDENTIFY GROWTH ENGINE

Don't do a deal until you understand the company's true engine of growth and are convinced the company has a "selling system" for acquiring customers and distributors.

Leading with Product not Opportunity

If I were writing this book early in my career, this distinction wouldn't have made my due diligence list. Today, with the channel's response to regulators and media concerns and the ever-increasing number of solo entrepreneur business opportunities, it is important that companies have a product-focused engine of growth.

When Amway, Melaleuca, Nu Skin, and Herbalife found their first wave of success in the United States, they were primarily selling a "business opportunity," and doing so in an environment where the term "side-hustle" hadn't yet been invented. The internet's evolution and increasing mobility have brought with it endless opportunities for solo entrepreneurs and made it less compelling to join a company just because it offers you the opportunity to earn part-time and then full-time income.

Today's direct selling success stories are focused on first convincing prospects of their consumer value, and then helping them to see how their products create an opportunity for those who share them. This evolution not only shows the channel's responsiveness to current market opportunities, but it also lends itself to a long-lasting business. In time, companies that focus on opportunity find it increasingly difficult to deliver on their distributor income promises. However, it is not difficult for companies with great products to continue to meet their customer's expectations, and loyal customers generate the revenues to in turn keep distributors more satisfied.

Product-first Direct Selling Unproven Internationally

It should be noted that this product-focused approach has been proven in the United States, but the largest U.S. companies have a majority of their sales in foreign markets and most of these businesses followed an opportunity model to gain that business. One might argue that in Asia markets especially, the opportunity message still resonates. The channel still waits to see a product-focused company that has seen significant traction and long-term sales internationally.

Product Quality and Value

Perhaps it goes without saying, but if a company is relying on its products to drive customer loyalty and repeat sales, then the product's quality needs to be able to sustain the value at the company's price point. As basic as this observation may be, there are too many investors who make the assumption that company revenues are the best proxy for judging product value. When asked what he would have done differently as part of his due diligence, a former executive of one of the channel's most spectacular failures said, "I would have looked at the product. I don't know how much due diligence they did on the product. I think products matter in this industry. I think products matter in terms of what makes them unique and different ... I think it matters what the competition looks like ... I think if they would have done any due diligence on [the products, they would have seen] that they were overpriced ... we had less than one percent of the revenue coming from a true customer base. If you were not being sold on the opportunity to make millions of dollars in that deal, you weren't buying this product. You just weren't."

Due Diligence Tip #5: LEAD WITH PRODUCT

Don't do a deal with a company whose meetings and recruiting events lead with the opportunity. Long term success in the United States comes to those companies whose first focus is on selling product and generating loyal customers.

Chapter 6

Due Diligence in the Field

Recently I learned of a private equity-owned company that had grown to nearly $500 million in sales and was known as the leader in their industry. Not long after investing in the company, the private equity owners replaced the CEO and eventually most of the management team. The new CEO had no experience in direct selling and was convinced that their clients were loyal to the company (not to the salesperson who had sold the service years before). He was also convinced that the direct selling sales field could be replaced with a more productive corporate-led sales and marketing effort. The CEO was wrong. The sales and marketing team they hired produced little incremental sales, and not nearly enough to make up for the hundreds of millions of lost sales that followed the direct sellers who left after hearing the CEO's plan to replace them.

This CEO learned the hard way that a direct sales company's sales force is its single most important asset and that there is a reason many call it "relationship marketing." Given the value of the sales force, investors should make a concerted effort to understand this asset and to feel confident that it will continue to perform.

In this chapter, we will help you understand the sales force and teach what to look for in assessing the health of the field. We will also provide suggestions on how you might gather information to make an informed decision about the quality of a sales force. From time to time, there are unforeseen issues or management mistakes that can have a significant negative impact on a direct selling company, but more often than not those who know what to look for will argue that they could have easily predicted the eventual collapse of a company. The following are practices that will help you become forewarned before you invest in a company that might have a fickle field sales force.

Growth: Organic or by Acquisition?

Most of us are used to the practice of hiring an executive recruiter to find great talent—often in the ranks of a competitor—to help fill a gap in our management team. Therefore, it is natural to assume the process would be similar when looking to grow a direct selling company. Why not start by recruiting top leaders with experience from other companies?

Believe it or not, while this has been done by most companies for many years, including direct selling companies who are filling corporate jobs, finding distributors from other companies has not been a practice widely accepted in the channel. It is, however, a common characteristic of companies that have a sudden and significant decline in sales. LifeVantage may be the first public company to openly invest in leadership acquisition via their Red Carpet program (more about their program and the logic behind it later). For the most part, companies have been hesitant to practice growth by acquiring leaders from other companies for four reasons:

- **Loyalty**
- **Duplication**
- **Impact on Leaders**
- **Erosion of Credibility**

Loyalty

Leaders who are willing to leave other companies to join your company are also more likely to leave your company to join someone else. While this is not always the result of such programs, the tragically fast failure of MonaVie and the publicly reported fall of formerly Blythe-owned ViSalus Sciences are examples of companies whose growth by acquiring leaders unraveled nearly as quickly as it was built.

In an interview with a senior executive with experience in more than one direct selling company, I learned that there are actually groups or "blocks" of distributors that brand themselves and go in masse from one company to another, often joining more than one company at the same time. This activity is more common in some foreign markets; Korea is especially well-known for it.

"If you don't have substance in your product, you don't have substance in the comp plan," this executive warns. "You're not really building an organic business, ... and [you're] acquiring leaders, and bringing big blocks of distributors in ... there is a massive risk with that kind of thing. Because they're not sticky. A lot of these groups have established their own brands. They don't want to over-align themselves with one company. So how sticky is that?"

Too often, investors see the immediate results of an MLM leader's first few months at a new company and begin to project growth at that rate going forward. Deals are done, debt is issued, and repayments promised, only to discover months later that the company's growth was simply a temporary structure that eventually was packed up and carted off to another company with a better offer.

Duplication

"Duplication" is a word you may hear often among direct selling executives and field leaders. It basically describes the process of growing by copying the activities and practices of those who have achieved the success you desire. In direct selling, a company hopes to have leaders that can duplicate their success by teaching new sales agents to do what they did. When leaders are acquired and given special payments, or are awarded a team of distributors, or earn a title or success in any way other than that path you expect a new sales agent to duplicate, sustainable growth rarely results. A company can prop up growth for a while, but the true economics and organic growth may not happen unless the acquired leaders first learn what it takes to succeed selling the company's specific products and business opportunity.

One example of the failure of duplication happened when Beachbody started its direct selling division Team Beachbody. The company began by recruiting many of its most loyal infomercial customers and a few "experienced" network marketers. To sweeten the deal, the company agreed to give these early distributors customers and leads acquired via their infomercial business. Many of these early distributors describe receiving checks without really knowing what they did to earn them. On paper, the company's new business looked like a success. Team Beachbody showed growth in distributors, customers, and sales, but very little of this growth was coming from the activities of these new distributors. In fact, in 2009, when the company stopped feeding customers into Team Beachbody and left the distributors on their own to recruit their own teams, sales dropped by nearly 50%. Not only did the company's growth stop, but sales declined because existing distributors (many of whom had success in previous direct selling companies) had never learned how to build a team at Beachbody. When I was hired to lead this division in 2010, I focused the team on creating a simple system to attract new customers and eventually to convert successful customers into coaches (or distributors). With a sales system to duplicate, Team Beachbody began to grow again from a low of $3 million a month to more than $60 million a month during my tenure.

Impact on the Leaders

Too often, the practice of recruiting leaders entices independent distributors to leave a profitable business they have worked long and hard to create by promising returns and payouts that never materialize. At least one billion-dollar global company allegedly uses a program to recruit leaders to grow their business; however, the leaders they recruit most often are tragic losers. This company allegedly has developed a formula that informs them how much they can pay a leader to join their company, how many distributors from the leader's former company they were likely to get, and how to create a hurdle just large enough that in the end the "lump sum payouts" promised to these leaders would never be paid out. The results are impressive for the company, but these leaders, who often left long and steady incomes at their previous companies, lose. They are left earning much less income (sometimes no income) and often have nothing to show for all of their life's work within a year of joining the new company.

Erosion of Credibility

Too often, companies who "acquire leaders" do so using special deals (signing bonuses, guaranteed commission amounts, leads, etc.) that are not available to most distributors and even attempt to hide these deals from the rest of the field. There are no secrets in a channel that was created to grow via word of mouth marketing. Other distributors will find out about the deals and often conclude that the playing field isn't fair, and that without a special deal they have no chance of becoming a top income earner at the company.

One leader, a respected financial advisor and a former CFO and controller to two large direct selling companies warns, "If you're investing in a private company, I would specifically look for special deals. And if you find any, walk away. It should just be disqualifying, not only because they're toxic but because they're emblematic of the founder's sense of fairness."

This leader, who asked not to be identified, was brought in by a private equity investor to be the CFO of a direct sales business that was the talk of the channel at the time because of its rapid rise to reported sales of more than $700 million. The leader said that the company had made a practice of using these deals to attract leaders and encourage them to bring their organizations from other companies. Looking back, the leader admits this practice should be a due diligence focus of investors.

"It would be tough to imagine [the company] ever achieving its glory without the special deals," the person said. "But it's also true that it's easy to imagine it surviving if it hadn't done them."

When asked how to identify whether a company has special deals, the former CFO said it is simple: "Ask the CEO and the CFO. If you have any doubt, ask to see the detail of the weekly/monthly compensation payout. Every company has some corrections from time to time, but manual payments of large amounts or leaders who leave other companies to join and then achieve high ranks in record time can often be signals that a special deal was made."

The Argument for Acquiring Leaders

When I set out to write this book, I brought with me a bias against any type of leadership acquisition program. I couldn't think of an example when it had worked. I had turned down leaders who had come to me at my former companies asking for a "bridge" or "package" to join our company and to bring leaders with them. In my opinion, this type of recruiting was the source of all ills in our channel and something that should not only be avoided but should also be outlawed by the Direct Selling Association's Code of Ethics.

During the course of my research, I was introduced to the LifeVantage Red Carpet program by the company's CEO, Darren Jensen. Darren, a smart long-time student of the channel, has become convinced that too many companies like LifeVantage have growth that outpaces their ability to develop enough leaders to sustain the number of new distributors recruited. LifeVantage experienced this type of rapid growth. By the time Jensen took over as CEO, the company found itself with impressive sales and tens of thousands of distributors, but far too few field leaders to help mentor the distributors who had joined during the company's hypergrowth. To solve this leadership gap, LifeVantage developed a program to make the company attractive to experienced leaders who fit a very specific profile. Jensen said that LifeVantage is looking for "younger, more technology driven people who are internet savvy, who know social media really well ... we focus our efforts on people who fit our culture."

When asked to contrast the Red Carpet program to the type of "special deals" described above, Devin Thorpe said that public programs that are out in the open are arguably part of the compensation plan. While he doubted the efficacy of these programs, Thorpe challenged me to find public disclosure of the deal. That wasn't hard to do. LifeVantage has talked openly about the Red Carpet program and has reported on it to its investors and included the program's cost in their public accounting. Here are a few bullet points describing the Red Carpet program taken from a presentation prepared for shareholders:

Recently deployed as an enhanced effort to attract new experienced leaders to LifeVantage through a program focused on creating relationships with developed leaders with access to our corporate leadership team, while providing activity-based incentives as they build their business

Incentivize experienced sales leaders to attract and retain accomplished salespeople to drive our business

Focused on enhancing distributor base by attracting a second wave of leaders who are technology adept and social commerce savvy

History of success with similar programs, which have demonstrated significant return on investment.

LifeVantage CEO Darren Jensen said that he has learned who to look for, how to vet applicants and how to make sure they were able to prove themselves at LifeVantage.

"They start from the ground floor and work their way up," he said. "They legitimately come in and build strong businesses, grassroots. They aren't pulling over organizations. They come and build it and grow it. So, there is a lot of respect in the program."

LifeVantage has been successful in slowing the company's decline and has reported a record year since Jensen was appointed CEO, so there may be something to the company's Red Carpet program. It is still in its infancy and it will be interesting to follow LifeVantage's success with it over time.

Jensen's argument for the need for such a program, his thoughtful approach to implementing it in a way that at least acknowledges historical challenges with this type of activity, and the analytical rigor with which he has surrounded the program give me reason to withhold judgment and to hope for its success.

Organic Growth is Recommended

LifeVantage's experience aside, few of the proven companies that have sustained solid businesses for decades have acquired leaders—or if they have, they have not been public about their program. For the most part, their growth has come organically from distributors starting in the business with no special deal and no advantage over anyone else.

I sent an early draft of this book to a hand full of individuals with decades of experience and a deep knowledge of the history of direct selling and this section raised the greatest concern. Industry experts insisted that I make it clear that there has been more damage caused by the practice of recruiting distributors from other companies than value received.

Over and over again I hear solid and steady growth companies claim that they are building a sales force that by and large has never had direct selling experience in the past. Even though each of these organizations believes that they are "unlike most companies," I've learned that the ones that avoid the dramatic falls in our business are more alike than different. These winning companies grow by attracting new prospects with a system that converts customers to distributors and builds distributors into leaders.

Whether you agree or disagree with the practice of acquiring leaders or distributors from other companies, investors need to identify how a company is acquiring distributors to determine if the method is economically feasible and sustainable, and to make sure the distributors joining the company are loyal and productive. If a company is acquiring distributors from other companies as a component of growth—especially if they are making special deals—further due diligence is required.

Due Diligence Tip #6: DISTRIBUTOR ACQUISITION

Beware of companies that rely heavily on acquiring leaders from other companies or who receive a sudden boost from a single leader and team joining from another company.

The ideal company

- **Will show growth both in sales and in sponsoring by existing distributors, and**
- **Will believe that "most" of their distributors have little or no direct selling experience, and**
- **Will have a focus on and method of first selling products to customers and then converting loyal customers into distributors.**

Learning from Events

I asked the CEOs I interviewed for specific things they would do as part of their due diligence if they were looking to invest in a direct selling company, and many said they would attend one of the company's events. Of those who said that, most added that they would do it alone, without a company representative directing them when and where to attend. I endorse that advice. I believe that attending corporate events is such a valuable way to understand a company that I have made it a practice before accepting any new job with a direct selling company.

Those of us who have worked in this channel have learned that a company's true colors are revealed at events, and not always on stage. It's true that you can learn a lot about the company's values by seeing who is allowed on stage and what content is presented, but perhaps the most valuable learning comes from what you can observe off-stage in the attitude and vibe of the audience and the conversations that are taking place among the attending distributors.

So, attend a company-sponsored event before investing time or money in a direct selling company, but if that is not possible, find an event sponsored by a local distributor. Or, as a last resort, join a conference call, a webinar or watch social media coverage of an event. By whatever means you observe the event(s), try to identify:

The age of the sales force. A few financially-sound companies in our space have very difficult challenges ahead in the coming decades as they face the aging of their field. An aging sales force is a red flag.

The ambition of their sales force. Are their distributors devoted product lovers who are more about loyal product usage, or are they business builders who really want to grow the company? The ideal company will have a healthy mix of loyal product followers along with plenty of distributors who see that product as their vehicle for creating generational wealth.

The hope and optimism of the field. Every company will have moments of contrived enthusiasm in the meeting, but what's the energy in the hall before and after general sessions, and what are the topics of the hall conversations? Are attendees excited about the future and the introductions made by the company, or are they subdued, complaining or talking about changes that need to be made?

The culture of the company. Is the content full of hype, science or education?   What are the demographics of the attendees and do they have the credibility required to sell in what the company claims to be its target market? If being at the convention is hard for you and you don't relish the idea of attending another one, pass on the investment.

On-stage content (Product/Opportunity mix). Here is where you learn whether the company's true emphasis is on product or opportunity. Are the success stories about the company's product, the business opportunity, or both? Perhaps more importantly, are the success stories recent or from years past?

Again, a former financial executive for a direct selling company that could be a poster child for bad private equity decisions said this about what could have been learned if an investor had attended an event as part of their due diligence:

"You've got a business that is being built almost one hundred percent on the opportunity to make millions of dollars ... [the top leader] was baptizing people at events and he was promoting his tool sets and saying ... this is all about changing lives and making money. The product wasn't even discussed in any of the events ... this was one hundred percent being built on kind of this almost fickle sort of cult-like ... revivals that would happen all around the money-making opportunity ... *go to an event and find out how they're promoting the product.*"

Due Diligence Tip #7: ATTEND A COMPANY EVENT

Don't do a deal with a company until you've attended one of their events as an anonymous guest and have seen the company's true colors.

Social Media Equity

Social media has become an essential tool for most direct selling businesses. In fact, many companies now refer to themselves a "social sellers." Social Media Equity is the value of the content being shared about the company on social media and the reach the company has through its own social media accounts and through its distributors. From 2010-2015, companies like ViSalus, Beachbody and Younique rode the wave of social media growth and saw significant gains as a result of having selling strategies that tied directly to social media. The use of social media has become more widespread and with that ubiquity comes the need to assess direct selling companies on three fronts:

- **Reputation and social equity**
- **The company's dependency on short-term social media dynamics**
- **The source of the company's momentum (or lack of momentum)**

Reputation and Social Equity

Investors will want to employ social media listening technology to gain a basic measurement of a company's reputation on social media. Are you buying a business with no equity, with great conversations happening on social media, or is the general tone on social media negative? Even companies with little proactive activity on social media might be the subject of considerable chatter that's worth understanding.

In the past decade, many of the party plan companies have had a very difficult time dealing with the negativity of disgruntled distributors on these forums. Companies that have not learned how to maintain positive social groups have faced headwinds as new distributors are met with serious and frequent negative comments by longer tenured distributors.

In addition to checking publicly available social media content, it would be worthwhile to ask the company to give you access (even chaperoned access) to their private social media groups. Ask to see company-sponsored or -monitored Facebook and other private social groups created for the company's leadership, customers, and distributors. In private leadership groups, companies tend to allow more freedom of expression and you might expect these groups to be less positive. These groups—especially leader groups—may be the best place for you to understand issues the company might not discuss with you in fundraising forums. Don't be alarmed by less than positive discussions but do look to see if the company has leaders who are supporting the company and defending executives. Take note of the topics of concern and use them to lead follow-on discussions with management.

Social Media-Dependent Engine of Growth

A few companies have designed their sales system to be social media centric. For example, Younique used short "before and after" videos connected to social media via a sales widget the company developed. No system was more effective and more viral, and the company grew to more than $400 million in sales before receiving a $1 billion valuation and an investment from Coty, Inc. (COTY: New York). Beachbody also developed a sales system connected to Facebook that relied on the platform for prospecting, recruiting and administering its accountability groups.

Early on, both companies were thrilled with the success their social media strategies had delivered and as social media platforms became more popular, sales increased accordingly. However, in meetings with both management teams a few years into their growth, I started hearing about the challenges they were having as a result of changes made to the algorithms social media companies used to determine what content to show their users. These conversations exposed the challenges of connecting a business model to a system you don't control. When you have built your business on a third-party platform and that platform suddenly changes, you may also be required to suddenly change. Both

Beachbody and Younique have been forced to adapt. Though both companies are privately held, there is ample public evidence to lead one to conclude that they have not been able to adapt fast enough to maintain their growth rate.

Companies that develop sales systems to leverage social media can continue to ride waves of growth. However, companies that connect their sales systems to social media need to expect that the system will have to be replaced and should be constantly refreshing and renewing their strategy so that it doesn't become outdated.

Source of Momentum

Social media can be an excellent tool to identify the source of a company's momentum. Typically, a company will grow because they have tapped into public enthusiasm for their product and/or mission, or because the word on the street is that others are making money and they don't want to miss out. In my experience, understanding the source of momentum is critical because it will inform your growth strategy—or indicate the need for a strategy change. For example, if a company is growing primarily because of enthusiasm for the amount people who are earning, the company may decide to work on increasing product loyalty (by focusing on product quality) OR to prepare to open new markets where the business opportunity plays well (Asia versus Europe, for example).

It is also important to understand how much momentum a company currently has. One simple tool for gauging momentum is Google's Trend tool, which provides a chart of how often the company is mentioned in

Google search. While some legacy brands have very little movement in their trend lines, many companies founded in the past decade do show a trend line that seems to have some correlation with the company's performance.

Due Diligence Tip #8: STUDY SOCIAL MEDIA BRAND

Validate the company's reputation and social media equity; drop in on private groups to see what issues the distributors are concerned about; make sure the company's sales system is not naively connected with a short-term social media trend; and see what type of momentum the company has on social medi

Connect with the Company's Culture

In 2006, Mark Fields, who later became chief executive of Ford Motor Company, was reportedly the first to attribute the phrase "Culture eats strategy for breakfast" to Peter Drucker.[35] Whether that quip is true in mainstream business or not, it certainly is an accurate representation of the critical role culture plays in direct selling.

If you were to attend the annual conferences of ten direct selling companies, you would be surprised to find that all ten companies had a very different culture about them. Some company's events would be like high school pep rallies with the apparent focus being all about getting attendees motivated and excited. Other companies would take a scientific approach, almost like academic conferences. Some companies are full of youth and others more on the mature side.

Isagenix CEO Travis Ogden counsels investors to do due diligence beyond the financial statements.

"You can get a feel for cultures," Ogden said. "You can sense whether or not it's a culture with true purpose and meaning—a culture that people would want to be naturally engaged with—versus a culture of hype that feels a little slimy."

As an investor, the culture should matter to you in two meaningful ways: First, the culture should align enough with your firm's culture as to never lead you to feel embarrassed by the company's meetings or by the distributors who carry the brand flag, and second, the culture should be considered if you are expecting significant changes in the future.

---

[35] https://www.forbes.com/sites/andrewcave/2017/11/09/culture-eats-strategy-for-breakfast-so-whats-for-lunch/#1e59f8467e0f, accessed June 15, 2019.

Culture as a precursor to change is an important consideration if you are investing in a company with the expectation to make any of the following changes:

- **International Expansion**
- **New Technology Adoption**
- **New Product Categories**

International Expansion

More than one executive has expressed their frustration with their field's lack of interest in international development. While a few companies have successfully expanded into new international markets without the support of the field in their initial market, the most effective and efficient way to grow into new markets is to do so with the leaders in your current market forging the way. If your investment model supposes that the company will expand internationally, I would make sure there is ample evidence that the company's current leaders want to expand their business and/or have the language and/or skills to build an international business.

In my experience, if you don't have leaders who will go to new markets or who have relationships in those markets, then your probability of success is pretty low. Companies that have success internationally are those that first do a great job developing leaders in their current markets. For example, Nu Skin had tremendous success in Japan in the 80s and 90s, but that success came as a result of first growing among Japanese Americans, primarily in Hawaii.

I asked one of the channel's top consultants, Paul Adams, about the key to international expansion.

"I'm a total believer that the leadership needs to take you there, not you take the leaders there," he replied.

If that statement is true—and I believe it is—you'd better have leaders ready and willing to expand internationally, or a plan to develop leaders who will support your strategy.

New Technology Adoption

Even in this world of mobile connectedness, some direct selling companies have a culture led by strong personalities opposed to adopting new technology. I'm aware of at least two large direct selling companies that will never see tech-enabled sales. The leaders of these organizations are not interested and/or are vocally opposed to anything other than person-to-person live selling. If you are of the school of thought that one should "never say never," then at least be realistic about the amount of change management that will be required, and plan adoption more conservatively based on the cultural disposition of the field leaders.

New Product Categories

Many people think of direct selling as a channel of distribution that can absorb new products easily. In my experience, direct sellers are extensions of a brand with the complexity of their own individual interpretation of what that brand is and what it means.

For example, while at Origami Owl, we introduced a few natural oils to accompany a new charm with a unique disk that could absorb and carry oils and perfumes. While we thought this was an ingenious way to extend our product line (from sight only to sight and smell), some of our distributors rejected the new products and oils stating that they didn't enroll to sell oils; they joined to sell lockets and charms.

In other words, often distributors have joined a company because of a product or category of product and any changes may cause them to reevaluate their involvement. This intense product loyalty is one of the reasons that many companies keep products with slow sales. Distributors hate when companies discontinue products, and too many companies have not fought the battles to gain alignment and permission to keep only performing products in their offering.

If you are investing in a company with plans to make significant changes to the product line—even if leadership thinks they are improvements—be cautious in your assumptions. Distributors do not see themselves as retail stores with a self-interest in maximizing their offerings. They are often emotionally connected with individual products and/or the category the company was founded around. Unless the company has developed a culture of consistent and successful product replacement, beware of plans that would attempt to make those changes quickly.

Finally, when it comes to culture, investors should be aware that a few companies have grown with a tight connection to a religious movement. More than one company has held religious services as part of their annual convention and have had top leaders evangelizing and even baptizing at company-sponsored events. Without passing judgment on the appropriateness of mixing business and religion, investors should make sure they understand if the company has a significant religious connection and determine if that affiliation aligns with the culture they wish to support in a company.

Due Diligence Tip #9: CULTURAL ALIGNMENT

Make sure the company you're investing in has the culture you feel comfortable attaching your brand equity to, and that the culture has the capability of adapting to any changes you believe are critical to realizing your investment.

Chapter 7

Financial Due Diligence

During the first month of my friend's appointment to CEO of a direct selling company, he was asked to meet two executives from a large private lender who held debt secured by the assets of his company. The meeting was held in the lobby of a Marriott hotel and was billed as a quick introduction. My friend (we will call him Steve) sat at an elevated table out of the flow of traffic and waited for the two executives to emerge. Minutes later they arrived. The first was a man of average build and the other could have comfortably suited up as an NFL lineman. He was clearly the "heavy" in the conversation that would follow.

The two executives took their places at the table, the first one sitting next to Steve and The Hulk across from him. After a few pleasantries, they began to question Steve about the poor performance of the business he had just been hired to run. And then they gave him the real reason for this meet-and-greet.

"We believe that we were misled," said the first man.

"And if that's the case we intend to be made whole," said The Hulk.

Steve knew that the lenders were likely not going to see their loan repaid, but he also was convinced that there was nothing untoward done by the previous management or owners. He also knew that the downturn in sales had actually started before the transaction was closed, and so Steve turned to the banker next to him, who had led due diligence for the lender, and said, "I don't think you have a case, in part because this trend started before you closed. Surely you were paying attention to the business performance before you closed. You did the proper diligence, right?"

Within the month, the banker who had led diligence had a new job with a new financial institution and the lenders started the long process of trying to recapture some value in this company. Steve told me that had he been on the lending team, he would have anticipated the likelihood of this company experiencing a correction and would have suggested that at a minimum the owners be required to maintain cash in the business for 6 to 12 months before making distributions. Instead, these lenders misread the slowing sales as seasonal and now faced the possibility of losing tens of millions of dollars.

I assume that every reader of this book will have plenty of experience doing basic financial due diligence, so this chapter will focus on two mistakes specific to direct selling that most often lead to poor deals. The first is the channel-specific issue of how a compensation plan can dramatically impact a company's profits, and the second issue is a reminder that every successful company in this channel has experienced a slowdown in their rate of growth AND a decline in sales at some point in their history. Most of the companies worked their way through the decline and found their footing again, but recently the practice of leveraging companies with debt that anticipates continued growth has, in fact, made it difficult (and in some cases, impossible) for the companies to find their way back to growth.

Compensation Plan Sustainability

Lori Bush, the chair of New Avon's Board of Managers and former CEO of Rodan+Fields, has had the chance to study several direct selling companies in recent years. I asked her what her primary considerations would be if tasked to do due diligence for a direct selling investment. She said she would start by making sure the compensation plan is sustainable.

"I would ask: does the company have a sustainable revenue model?" she said. "Oftentimes the compensation plan isn't right. I've seen this happen, shockingly seen it happen, where a company starts to grow and mature and suddenly, they can't afford their compensation plan anymore ... you promote a really rich compensation plan, but then you can't afford it. ... There needs to be a very clear understanding of what kind of gross profit margin you need to support the compensation plan that you want or that you have, and what kind of contribution margin you need to cover your operating overhead and expenses."

For most direct selling companies, the compensation plan is the single most significant expense—by far—so getting the economics of the plan right is of utmost importance. Changing a company's compensation plan is possible, but it takes very careful consideration, lots of preparation, and robust communication between the company and its field leaders. To avoid the disruption of making changes to a compensation plan, make sure to review the economics of the company's compensation plan during your due diligence by asking the following questions:

- **Is the company paying all promised commissions and bonuses?**
- **Will leaders need to be paid more to remain motivated?**
- **Can you model the plan?**
- **Is the compensation plan effective in its current form?**
- **Is the compensation plan paying employees or owners?**
- **Is there a process for maintaining margin discipline?**

Let's explore each of these critical questions in depth.

Is the company paying all promised commissions?

Most mature compensation plans will have little variability from one pay period to the next (with the possible exception of short-term incentives the company might offer from time to time). In contrast, newer companies could see their payout increase in stairstep fashion because compensation plans do not pay all components of the plan in the first few years. As the company matures and sales agents grow their organizations and volume, they access additional bonuses and the payout increases. Even if a company has had a steady payout percentage, make sure you model every possible payout promised or considered.

Will leaders need more pay to remain motivated?

As companies mature, they often discover that their initial plan isn't robust enough to continue to keep leaders engaged. If sales agents are qualifying at their top level in the compensation plan, it is possible that the company will need to create new incentives for top leaders that often means an increase in the total cost of incentives.

Ask executives specifically if there are components in the compensation plan that are not being paid out at this time, or if they anticipate the need to add anything in the future. If the answer is "yes" to either question, make sure your financial model properly forecasts the fully loaded compensation plan.

Can you model the plan?

Although this seems like it would be simple, creating an accurate financial sensitivity model with some compensation plans is extremely difficult. I have spent tens of thousands of dollars on consultants with math degrees from the country's top universities and still did not have confidence in how one company's plan would pay out during extreme growth or decline. The plan that has given experts the most concern is the Binary compensation plan because of its tendency to have significant volume remain dormant (or unpaid) for a time only to see a distributor find a way to qualify for the latent commissions, triggering a sudden increase in payout.

Company executives should be able to build sensitivity models for most compensation plans. However, if there is any modeling risk, make sure there's enough margin to allow for a period of higher compensation until management is able to make the changes required to bring the plan back to feasibility again. Under the best of circumstances, it could take management 18 to 24 months to make corrections to a compensation plan.

Some plans, though difficult to model, have built-in rules that could be easily adjusted in the event that payout begins to increase unexpectedly. Management should be able to articulate the rules that can be adjusted to keep the compensation plan within an acceptable payout range. The rules could decrease the time required to make changes and allow a company to be more responsive to unexpected increases in their payout percentage.

Is the current compensation plan effective?

Throughout my years in the channel, I have had the opportunity to work on several compensation plans and have often turned to Mark Rawlins, Mitch Stowell and their team at InfoTrax to help me with detailed modeling and analysis. On their website, www.mlm.com, InfoTrax reminds us that "Good compensation plans are designed to reward the behavior that helps build and maintain product sales. Each compensation plan is composed of multiple commissions, each filling a different role, rewarding a different behavior. Companies need to understand the advantages to each type of commission and build a successful strategy that meets the needs of every type of distributor that will profit their organization."[36]

---

[36] https://mlm.com/category/compensation-strategy/, accessed May 24, 2019.

To make sure the compensation plan is complete in its current form, it is helpful to ask management to break down the purpose of each element of the plan. For example, a compensation plan should reward distributors for:

Selling products to new customers. This is typically rewarded via a retail sales commission (the difference between the wholesale price distributors pay for the product and the suggested retail price).

Recruiting new distributors. It is illegal to pay a commission just for recruiting, so most good plans will reward distributors with an override commission/bonus for sales made by distributors they recruit or sponsor. For example, if Jim sponsors Jill, Jim could earn 3% on all of the sales made by Jill.

Training/retaining distributors. Many plans have "leadership bonus" programs that provide a bonus pool that leaders can earn for building and maintaining large volumes of sales and a large number of team members.

Mentoring distributors to become leaders and progress through the plan. You want a plan that encourages leaders to develop other leaders, but there are times when this doesn't happen. For example, a "Breakaway" compensation plan can create situations where a team grows, but a leader's compensation declines because they have created a leader on their team who now earns part of the commissions that were being paid to them.

You can learn more about this type of plan (and how to overcome its weaknesses) online at InfoTrax's www.mlm.com website.

Are employees or owners earning as distributors?

In an interview with the Chairman and CEO (and investor) in one large company, I learned of another important question to ask in your due diligence: "Are any company executives, employees, owners or family members being compensated through the company's distributor compensation plan?"

This executive told me the story of a company he'd invested in.

"Four founders started the company, and every one of them had a downline," he explained. "Their salaries were two hundred thousand a year. I invested ten million and found out later that they were making four hundred thousand each off of the company's compensation plan. Now their combined salary is six hundred thousand a year, times four, and there's no money left. So, you've got to be able to know what their total take home is as part of your due diligence."

There are examples of legitimate companies that allow founders, owners, management, and employees to earn through the compensation plan. Some companies even require employees to be distributors, but investors have the right to understand the entire compensation being paid, both as salary and as incentives from the distributor compensation plan.

Is there a process for maintaining margin discipline?

Direct selling companies thrive on stability, not only in the compensation system created to reward distributors but also in product pricing. Often the two are linked so closely that one impacts the other. Most companies begin in the United States and give little thought to the future impact Forex will have on prices and margins when the company expands to new markets. It is also not uncommon for pricing to be controlled by marketing and/or sales with prices set on their opinion of what will move the most units. The best companies have created a process for pricing that allows consideration from multiple departments. These companies deploy a pricing model that prescribes the minimum margin needed to fund the compensation plan and still leave sufficient margin for the company to remain profitable. Left unattended, prices tend to be set without proper consideration for the full channel costs and profitability begins to slowly deteriorate over time. Make sure the company you are investing in has a disciplined and formal process for pricing or help them implement one when you become a partner.

Due Diligence Tip #10: MODEL "ALL-IN" COMP PLAN

Make sure the compensation expense in your model represents all of the announced and anticipated components of the compensation plan. Too often young companies have yet to reach the "full payout" that should be planned for in your economic models.

Expect Sales to Slow or Decline

Several of the channel's most notable private equity failures involved leverage obtained at the peak of sales and based on models that projected continued growth. Even great companies with decades of profitable returns have experienced cycles in their sales. Included at the end of this chapter are the revenue graphs of a few of the world's largest direct selling companies. As you review these revenue charts you will notice that all of these companies have experienced slowing and sales declines. In recent years, only USANA Health Sciences has been able to put together more than 15 years of steady growth.

Because of the channel's dependence on volunteer sales and organically-acquired field leadership, often revenues tend to outpace a company's ability to grow the field leadership or infrastructure to support continued "blitzscaling" for more than just a few years. LifeVantage CEO Darren Jensen described this challenge.

"Too many investors are attracted by a company in the 'pop phase,'" he said, "not knowing that as a rule of thumb it will only run for eighteen months or so, and then there's a one hundred percent probability that the company will either implode or that they will go through a glide or flat phase. They will see a flattening of the business or a slow downward glide while the underlying distributor leadership base catches up with the revenue."

Jensen explained that the news of the investment can often create enough uncertainty in the field to knock the company out of momentum or out of its blitzscale, and put it in (hopefully) a flat position that will probably run for a number of years until the leadership catches up. Patient investors who avoid creating more uncertainty with unnecessary changes in management will see the company develop the potential for another blitzscaling.

"The key is for investors to understand that a slowing, flattening and often a downward glide in sales is a predicable reaction to significant sales growth," Jensen added.

Knowing that no direct selling company will have continuous sales growth, former CEO and long-time direct selling executive Elizabeth Thibaudeau encourages investors to "plan for and anticipate that sales dips are going to happen." Far too often, companies are levered with repayment terms that can only be supported at the company's peak cash flows. With no room built into the model for a correction, the natural corrections that come will wipe out shareholder value first for the private equity owners, and often for the debt holders as well.

Due Diligence Tip #11: EXPECT SALES TO DECLINE

Make sure your economic model and any accompanying debt service can survive a slowing, flattening, or even a 10 to 30% decline in sales soon after the close of your investment.

Exhibit 1: Historical Revenue Charts

The charts below have been created using publicly available data either from the company's published public filings, news reports or both. In some cases, we have smoothed gaps in the charts where we have not been able to gather public data. One source informed me that Mary Kay's current sales are "considerably more than $3 billion," but he is not at liberty to speak publicly for the company and also would not provide specific sales numbers, so the chart below does not reflect what perhaps is a renewal or growth.

Natura:

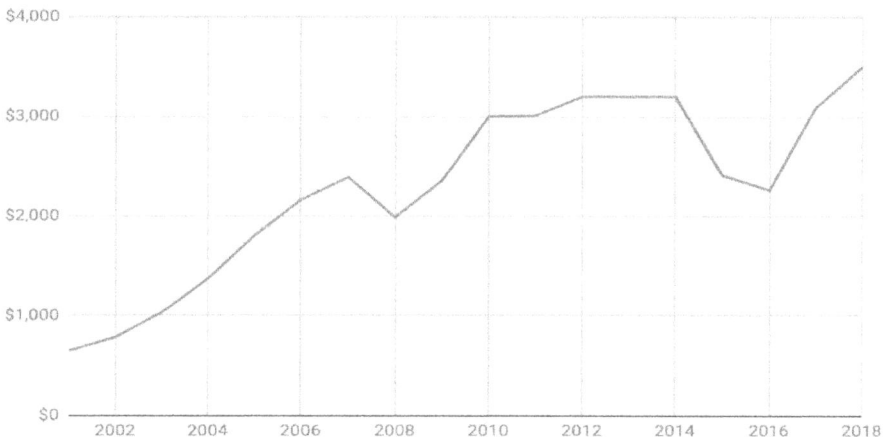

Nu Skin:

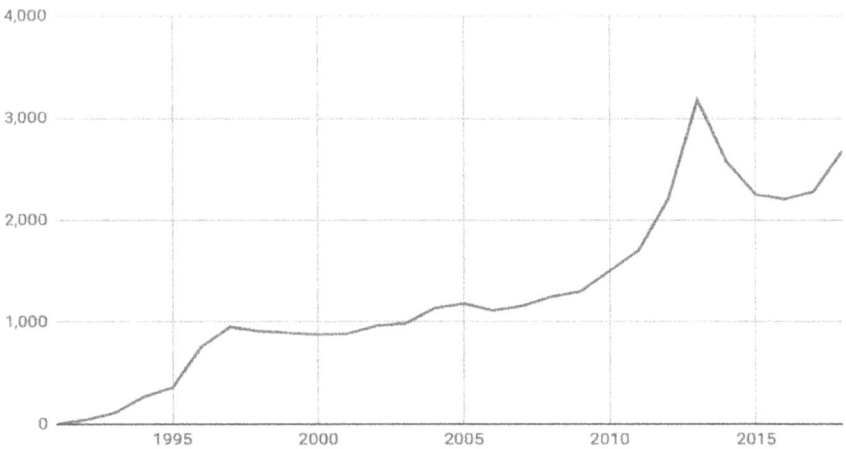

Herbalife:

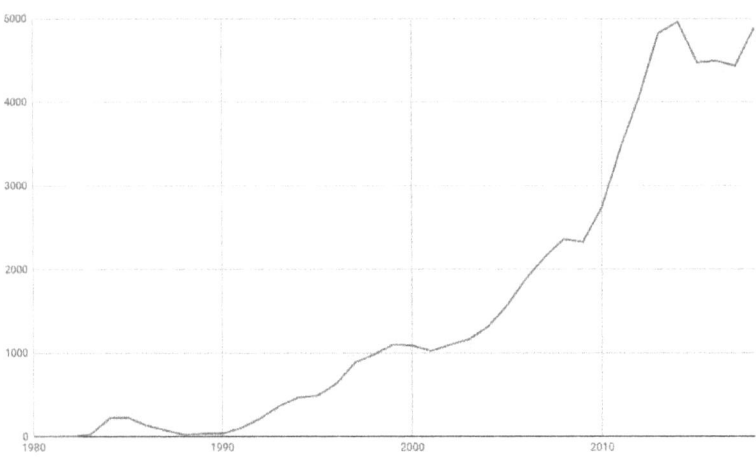

Mary Kay:

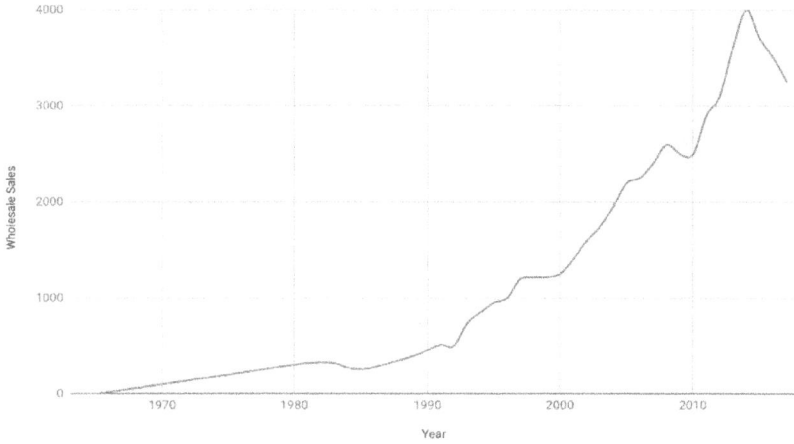

Amway:

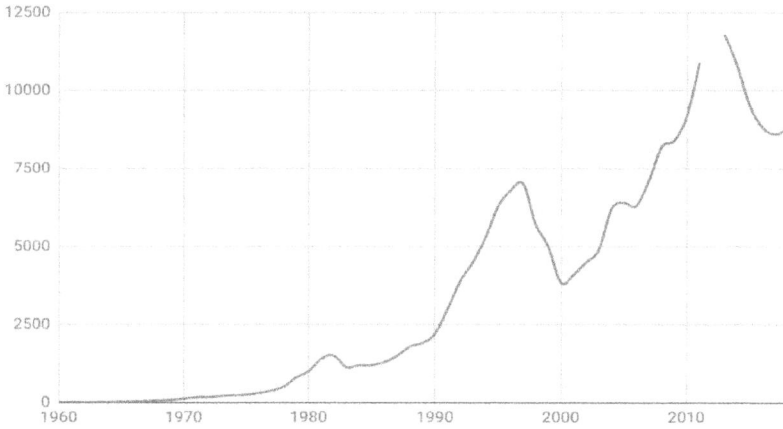

Avon:

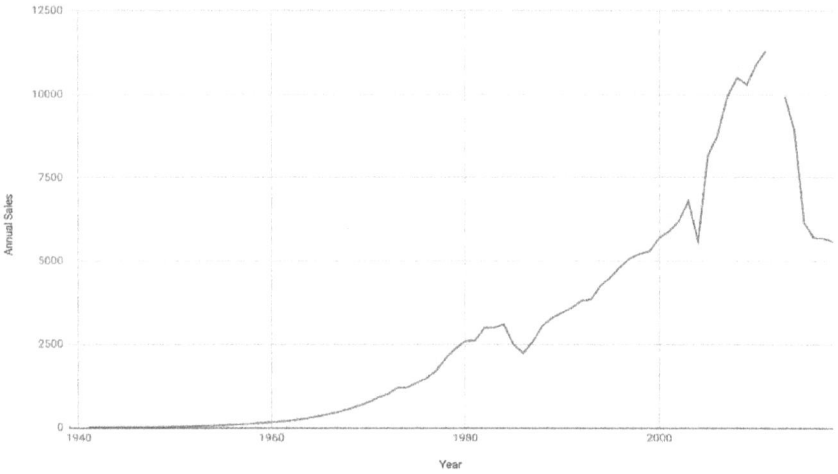

USANA Health Sciences:

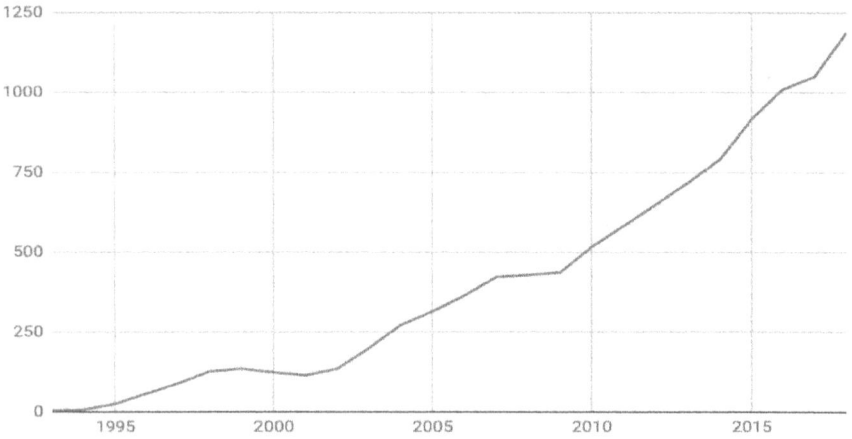

Exhibit 2: Due Diligence Tips Recapped

Due Diligence Tip #1: FOUNDER ALIGNMENT

Don't do a deal with a founder you don't trust and who doesn't have the self-awareness to accept the professional help you expect to provide.

Due Diligence Tip #2: ALIGN MANAGEMENT

Don't settle for poor management, and make sure the team has the necessary channel attitude and experience, a positive attitude toward direct selling, and is aligned in creating enterprise value.

Due Diligence Tip #3: REGULATORY RISK

Make sure the company's commissions only reward product sales, that the products are priced at a reasonable value, and that distributors are not relying on unsubstantiated product or income claims. If the company is doing business in international markets, make sure it has proper registrations as required by each country.

Due Diligence Tip #4: IDENTIFY THE TRUE GROWTH ENGINE

Don't do a deal until you understand the company's true engine of growth and are convinced the company has a "system" for acquiring customers and distributors.

Due Diligence Tip #5: LEAD WITH PRODUCT

Don't do a deal with a company whose meetings and recruiting events lead with the opportunity. Long term success in the United States comes to those companies whose first focus is to generate loyal customers.

Due Diligence Tip #6: DISTRIBUTOR ACQUISITION

Beware of companies that rely heavily on acquiring leaders from other companies or who receive a sudden boost from a single leader and team joining from another company.

Due Diligence Tip #7: ATTEND A COMPANY EVENT

Don't do a deal with a company until you've attended one of their events as an anonymous guest and have seen the company's true colors.

Due Diligence Tip #8: STUDY THE COMPANY ON SOCIAL MEDIA

Validate the company's reputation and social media equity; drop in on private groups to see what issues the distributors are concerned about; make sure the company's sales system is not naively connected with a short-term social media trend; and see what type of momentum the company has on social media.

Due Diligence Tip #9: CULTURAL ALIGNMENT

Make sure the company you're investing in has the culture you feel comfortable attaching your brand equity to, and that the culture has the capability of adapting to any changes you believe are critical to realizing your investment.

Due Diligence Tip #10: MODEL THE "ALL-IN" COMPENSATION EXPENSES

Make sure the compensation expense in your model represents all of the announced and anticipated components of the compensation plan. Too often young companies have yet to reach the "full payout" that should be planned for in your economic models.

Due Diligence Tip #11: EXPECT SALES TO DECLINE

Make sure your economic model and any accompanying debt service can survive a slowing, flattening, or even a 10 to 30% decline in sales soon after the close of your investment.

Chapter 8

This is Not Traditional Retailing

In 2016, the Direct Selling Association (DSA) claimed that the channel made up just 0.73% of all retail sales. According to the DSA's 2017 Growth & Outlook Report, "Direct retail sales as a percentage of overall retail sales in the U.S. have remained fairly consistent over the past six years, accounting for roughly three-quarters of 1% of total retail sales. This shows that direct selling has the potential to grow by taking market share from other forms of retail."[37]

Despite the DSA's effort to categorize direct selling as part of the retail sales total and acknowledging the fact that direct selling competes for consumer's retail dollars, it's not wise for investors to apply traditional retail metrics to direct selling companies. Over and over again the executives I interviewed reminded me that "direct selling is not like traditional retailing." In fact, when I asked the executives what mistakes those outside the channel most often make when analyzing a direct selling company, all of them replied that those outside the channel fail to

---

[37] 2017 Growth & Outlook Report, DSA

understand the critical differences between direct selling and brick-and-mortar retail selling.

Winfield Consulting CEO Jim Northrop put it this way:

They have a template that they apply, which is the same template they would use if they were to buy a retail store or wholesaler-to-retailer. The direct sales model is completely dynamic. And what does that mean? Well, it thrives on new people and developing a portion of those new people to be team builders who attract other people. And those people have a life cycle on their own so that you have to be in the business of continually replenishing with new distributors who in turn become new leaders who would, in turn, sustain your business.

Now that's very different than a business where you open a store and then you're able to look at same-store sales and evaluate whether your business is solid or not predicated on whether your same-store sales are growing or declining. And that's the natural tendency for ninety percent of the private equity firms or more, to say, we will just evaluate these companies this way.

When asked to be specific about how direct selling differs from brick-and-mortar retailers, the executives came up with five primary ways:

Relationships

Key Performance Indicators

Saturation

Leader-led Expansion

Capital Doesn't Drive Growth

Relationships

Customers and distributors are not "nameless" or "masses." They are friends who know and are known by members of the corporate team. These relationships bring with them all of the advantages and challenges of human dynamics and make almost every decision more complicated than the "transactional," as in retail. For example, changing out management in a direct selling company could motivate a few or a lot of distributors to stop selling or to leave the company altogether, while most retail customers could care less about the management of the firm.

Those new to the channel often assume that distributors will eventually support a decision as long as it is logical and built on sound reason and analysis. Unfortunately, that is not always true. This is a lesson I learned the hard way—through experience. As a new CEO at a fashion jewelry business, I was struck by the frustration so many of the distributors expressed on the company's private Facebook page, and assumed that I could resolve many of those frustrations by spending time responding to several of the posts. So, I set aside an hour one afternoon and invited distributors to join me on Facebook for a question and answer period. The distributors on this page were very excited leading up to the Q&A session. I expected it to be filled with some tough questions, but overall planned on winning over everyone with my openness and candor. For more than four hours, I sat reading and responding to posts, typing as fast as I could and bouncing between threads on the page. I have conducted live Q&A for years with positive outcomes every time. My undefeated record was shattered on this day, though. Here's just one painful excerpt:

Question: *"Why would the company pay more to some distributors and less to others for selling the same thing?"*

Answer: *"Everyone has the chance to earn the same amount, but we believe it is fair to reward those who sell more with a higher commission rate."*

Response: *"I disagree. I have been with this company for a long time and have tried as hard as anyone. It is not fair to pay someone more just because they are lucky enough to have more sales and to pay me less because I'm not so lucky. Nobody has worked harder than me."*

I'll spare you the ongoing dialogue and additional examples similar to this but suffice it to say that many direct selling companies have attracted distributors with no previous business experience. Many of these distributors are successful; some are just loyal, but many have a very different logic than the "reward results not effort" capitalism many business leaders follow.

For many, their motivation and involvement are centered on their emotional experience with the company, not the rational calculus of how they will earn money. The fact is that most companies fail if they never tap into the emotion of their sales field, and once they have tapped into that emotion, they must respect it when making decisions.

Several years ago, I noticed that many top leaders who had achieved success beyond their wildest dreams were becoming less trusting of their company over time. I began a series of interviews with these leaders to try to understand this phenomenon. Finally, a meeting with one leader provided me a critical insight. She told me how she had started in a call center making a modest hourly income. Her life had changed dramatically since she joined the company as a distributor—at the time we were talking she was making more than $700,000 a year. She told me how grateful she was, and then she said something that really opened my eyes.

"Don't get me wrong, I appreciate what I have," she said, "but *I never want to work that hard again*."

Another leader in the same company gave me an additional keen insight.

"It's terrifying when I stop and think about the fact that an executive here could radically impact my income by making a decision with no input from me," he said. "That makes me feel very helpless."

For those of us with a corporate salary, it is fairly easy to make a change and expect to replace and perhaps improve our salary. For those with no previous experience, who have built a team and earned a large income from scratch, the opportunity to replace that income elsewhere seems impossible—or at the very least, not desirable. These top leaders begin to realize how dependent they are on the company they represent and the management of that company. They realize that their earnings can be significantly impacted by things totally beyond their control. Given this fear, many top leaders become more risk averse for fear that any changes made by the company could significantly impact their income and lifestyle. This fear often is interpreted by management as being "negative" or "emotional" rather than grateful and logical.

While retailers have a large human resource element to their businesses and all of the human dynamics that accompany an employee base, their human relationships are contractual, and they choose whom to employ. Direct sellers rely on a total volunteer salesforce who join by their own election. Direct sellers are not hired, they choose to sell for a company and continue to sell on their own terms (much like a volunteer). There are no interviews, no screenings and no opportunity to require certain training or previous experience. One direct selling CEO said that she felt like her job was part psychologist, part public speaker and motivator, and the other part business leader. As you become an advisor to a direct selling company, realize that there is always a significant relationship and emotional side to every decision. Great companies honor those relationships and take the extra time to address both the head and the heart of any significant change planned.

Saturation

Saturation is a concern when building out a brick-and-mortar retail company and is easily measured using population statistics and a mathematical model that can help guide retailers' decisions. Given the fact that direct selling accounts for the extraordinarily small percentage (just 0.73%) of the total retail market, there is probably not a single direct selling company that has actually experienced true saturation. Facts aside, there are plenty of companies that have seen their sales slow or decline because their field perceived the market was saturated. Saturation in direct selling is less quantitative and more of a qualitative opinion among sales representatives, and it must be managed.

Direct selling distribution builds without a master plan, but instead follows the relationships of the sales force. The friend-to-friend nature of selling can lead to a dense population of distributors and customers in a single city or suburb and few, if any, in some states. Often, fashion direct sellers will begin to hear top distributors talk about "saturation" only because it seems like everyone they know has purchased or declined to purchase the product. When a person goes to work and more than one person is wearing the same thing, the seed that things are becoming saturated is sown. This perception of saturation can lead to a loss of momentum and a perception that the company is no longer a great business opportunity, when in fact that may only be true in a few zip codes.

Fighting the perception of saturation is a key challenge, especially for fast growth, semi-durable goods companies. In one such company, I produced a series of charts showing that in the 35,000 or so active zip codes in the US, the company had no customers in more than 25,000 zip codes, and still the perception of saturation persisted!

This problem with micro-saturation in an otherwise wide-open market may be one reason why direct sellers who offer products like home decor, fashion jewelry, bags, cookware, and candles have approached but been unable to sustain sales over one billion dollars. This is less of an issue for companies with consumable products—something that customers and distributors will use up quickly and want to reorder next month. Semi-durable goods like jewelry, clothing or bedding have less customer reorders and therefore need to increase the number of customers faster than a consumable company would for the same unit sales.

Helping companies make investments in programs that will facilitate leapfrogging beyond their current network of relationships into new markets and new friend groups can be a meaningful way for investors to add value to their direct selling portfolio companies. This is not a skill developed, taught or talked about much in the channel and may be the missing link to helping many semi-durable goods companies break the billion-dollar barrier.

Leader-led Expansion

Unlike a traditional retail business, direct selling companies don't attack geographies with a map. They are not able to identify white space in a specific state or region and decide that they will open operations there next. Direct selling companies don't have the ability to tell the field what to do or where to sell. They only have influence on their field. Looking at geographical white space, whether in the U.S. or internationally, might be a sign of opportunity, but it isn't as formulaic as it would be if working with a brick-and-mortar retailer.

Direct sellers exploit white space opportunity only if they are able to find volunteers from within the current distributor base with relationships in the areas they hope to grow. In other words, too often companies open a new market expecting to have sales success without having leaders who are interested in building in that new market. The great international success stories most often include local success among current distributors with contacts in the targeted markets. For example, in one of my interviews, I learned of a company that had only opened one market—the Philippines. They were having amazing success; in fact, that market was growing to be larger than their U.S. market.

"Why did you choose to go to the Philippines of all places?" I asked.

"Because we had strong leaders and solid success among Filipinos in the U.S., and they took us there," was the answer.

While investors and company executives like to believe they are in charge and can direct the geographic expansion of a direct selling company, the most successful companies are those working with their current field leaders and developing diverse distributors in their current markets, and then allowing their leaders to lead them to new geographies.

The company can deploy capital to invest in support for markets with languages they want to grow. For example, they can translate materials into Spanish and hire a Spanish speaking sales executive as part of an effort to find and develop Spanish speaking leaders with relationships to take them into Latin America. But clearly this "if we build it, they will come" strategy is much different than making a choice to open retail stores in an untapped market.

When we reference 'leader-led' international expansion, it is essential to note that we are not saying that a company should open any market in which their top leaders claim to have contacts. Too many companies have destroyed their profitability and reputation, chasing leader's international expansion whims. My definition of leader-led global expansion includes a thoughtful business analysis of where to go that includes a substantial weighting of those markets where the company's current leaders have language skills, contacts or are reasonably confident in their ability to find connections, and a willingness to travel and work in the market.

Capital Doesn't Drive Growth

Too often, investors believe that the capital they invest in a direct selling company will be deployed in activities that will have an immediate impact on sales. Why wouldn't that be true? In the retail channel, capital is deployed to open new points of distribution, to fund advertising or to launch a new product line and in each case, proper market research will ensure a direct return on the capital invested. Such is not the case in direct selling.

Conversely, capital invested in direct selling companies rarely produces such a predictable return. The difficulty in effectively employing cash is a reason many public direct selling companies chose to invest their cash in share buyback programs. Dave Wentz said that USANA spent over $2 billion on their share buyback program in the 20 years following Y2K because it wasn't easy to find ways to deploy cash with a predictable return.

Several of the CEOs I interviewed would advise not investing in a direct selling company expecting that capital alone will have an impact. Cash is critical for early-stage companies, but most of the time capital in later stage companies is primarily focused on making changes to the CAP table[38]. Even international expansion, which can be quite capital intensive for most companies, can be a minimal expense for direct sellers. Some may choose to invest in an office, in hiring a head of sales or invest in pre-launch marketing, but most companies only have product registration

---

[38] A **cap table** (or capitalization table) is a **table** providing an analysis of a company's percentages of ownership, equity dilution, and value of equity in each round of investment by founders, investors, and other owners.(SOURCE: Wikipedia)

fees, legal and organization fees, travel, rent and the need for a few employees. Capital for expansion is rarely a requirement for companies in this channel.

While most of the CEOs I interviewed agreed with Wentz on the relatively low capital needs of the channel, at least one CEO, Beachbody's Carl Daikeler, felt it important to deploy capital to keep up with the advances in technology.

"In a world where we are competing with Amazon for attention and performance, and execution, and technology, anybody who's not investing in technology and trying to look farther down the field is going to find that their distributor base all of a sudden starts to get very top heavy as it relates to age," Daikeler said. "You need to stay relevant technologically to stay appealing to the next generation that's coming up. We have to keep investing in technology. We have to keep investing in being competitive with people who don't have the compensation plan pressure that we have."

Daikeler admitted that there was not the type of direct return investment opportunities that investors might find in other industries, where you can acquire another company and benefit from scale. He also acknowledged that "all technology and all innovation has a risk to it, and it's difficult to get a predictable ROI, but we're in a space where I think there's still room for dramatic, like *really* dramatic growth, and we're going to have to continue to invest in it to find that sweet spot."

Key Performance Indicators

Too often investors attempt to apply retail metrics to direct selling. One common mistake is to use a "same-store sales" analysis with the logic that individual sellers (like stores) should become more productive over time. In fact, the reality is almost exactly the opposite of that theory. The best distributors do have a period of increased sales (in some models), but personal sales decline over time as the most successful distributors begin to spend more time mentoring and developing new sellers and less time on their personal sales volume. The chart below shows what a successful distributor's productivity might look like as they move from personal sales to building and mentoring a team.

Time Selling and Time Mentoring

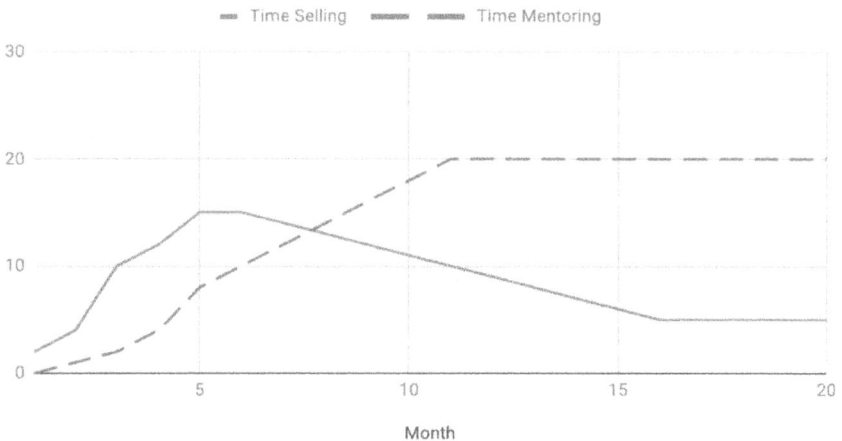

Month

Sometimes sales can also be a misleading Key Performance Indicator (KPI) as it's possible for companies to have increasing sales even as the new customer/distributor count is declining (signaling declining sales in the future). In an interview with the CEO of a direct selling company that had been the sweetheart of the channel, he told me that his business had been in decline for more than a year. This gentleman (who asked to remain nameless) said that his biggest regret was that he had ignored the signs of decline because sales had continued to climb even though new customer and distributor enrollments had fallen.

"I let the sales numbers fool me into thinking things were fine," he said. "I didn't realize until it was too late that the sales growth had shifted from more customers buying to fewer customers buying more."

Sales alone is a poor way to assess the health of a direct selling company. To help guide investors, I have included a few recommended KPIs that you could review prior to an investment or implement as part of your oversight role. These KPIs, with a short definition of each suggested measure, can be found at the end of this chapter and also on our website at www.investingindirectselling.com.

Make sure that your target company is able to validate that the information they are gathering is defined accurately and collected properly. I interviewed one consultant who emphasized the challenge many companies have in producing accurate data. This consultant (who is not mentioned to protect his relationship with the client) warned:

"I was asked to consult with a company that had sales or more than half a billion dollars and was surprised by how little data they had. They couldn't produce reports on all sorts of things that should be readily available. And then, when I did get reports, we found out later they were all wrong."

Make sure you choose relevant KPIs and validate the accuracy of the data you are receiving early in your partnership with your new portfolio company.

While direct sellers compete for retail dollars, the business model is different enough to warrant its own KPIs, channel-specific consideration on change and change management and more of an indirect ROI expectation with regards to the deployment of capital. I have gathered and prioritized the KPIs below (Exhibit 1) to provide readers insight into what information should guide their review of a direct selling company.

Exhibit 3: Direct Selling KPIs

The following are KPIs direct sellers should track in their business, in their order of importance.

Sales Performance

Net Active Distributors: The number of distributors who have personally produced volume or recruited new customers/distributors in the last month.

Customers: The number of people without a distributor agreement who placed an order with the company in the last month.

Advancement

Number of Rank Advancements: Total distributors who advanced to a new rank.

Time to Each Rank: How many months (or paid periods) it takes to reach a rank in the compensation plan.

Paid at Rank as % of Total at Career Rank: This KPI compares the current rank distributors qualify at (or paid rank) versus their highest rank or career rank. NOTE: most companies allow someone to keep the title of the highest rank they've earned even if they aren't currently qualifying at a rank and call that rank their career rank.

Time at Highest Rank: Measuring how many months (or pay periods) the average person maintains their highest rank is helpful to understand how solid the organizations are being built.

Net Promoter Score: A simple one question survey, administered on a consistent basis, that simply gives you directional data on the field's enthusiasm for sharing your products. Administering this by cohort can give you even more valuable data over time. The Net Promoter Score asks customers and distributors to answer the following question using a ten-point scale (0 = Very Unlikely, 10= Very Likely): *"Considering your complete experience with our company, how likely would you be to recommend us to a friend or colleague?"*

Cohort Data

Separate all distributors from all customers who join each month and put each group of distributors into a cohort to help you measure the effectiveness of your programs over time. Track each cohort against these variables over time:

Personal Volume: How much volume is each new customer/distributor purchasing/selling?

Sponsoring

Number/percent of each cohort sponsoring.

The number of new customers and/or distributors being sponsored by each cohort per month/pay period.

The frequency of sponsorship among those who are sponsoring.

Retention

Percentage of Cohort Active: Comparing cohort active in month x, y, z, etc. against all previous cohorts.

Distributor Earnings

Gives management insight from a distributor's perspective.

Number of New Distributors Earning – new could be defined by the company based on their selling system (typically less than 90 days).

Total Cash Paid in Commissions – this is a simple way to see if your opportunity is growing or declining.

Average Monthly Earnings by Rank

Number of Earners at Defined Benchmarks (my suggestions are below)

Earning ($1): How many distributors earned anything in a pay period?

Earning Enough to Pay for Product: If someone is earning enough to pay for the product, you would assume they would never leave.

Earning Fun Money ($200, $300, $500): Several companies believe that $300 a month will keep a distributor for life.

Earning Part-Time Income ($1000, $1500)

Earning Full-Time Income ($5K-$10K): Does your opportunity allow distributors to leave a full-time job and work their business full-time?

Marketing Performance

I believe the marketing department should be responsible for increasing the average order size per customer and support the distributor's efforts to acquire new customers. Measures of marketing success might include:

Subscription Sales

Subscription as Percent of Total Sales: What percent of the company's total sales are being ordered as part of a subscription (or auto-ship/back-up order)?

Average life per subscription: How many consecutive orders does the average subscriber receive before they cancel their subscription?

Average Order Size: Most often measured in dollars per order but could also include total products per order.

Customer Orders: Orders sold to purchasers without a distributor agreement.

Distributor Orders:

> ***Personal use:*** Product being purchased by distributors for their personal use.
>
> ***Retail Sales:*** To customers from distributor's inventory (if possible).

Operations Performance

Time to Fulfill Order: The ideal is to measure the time from receipt of order until the customer receives the order, but often it is more feasible to measure time from order received to time order leaves the warehouse.

Order Accuracy: Can be measured as a percent of items picked, but it's more meaningful to measure the percentage of orders that had an error.

Orders per Payroll Dollar: Good way to keep labor in line and discourage too much management versus product labor in the warehouse.

Chapter 9

Creating Shareholder Value

In 2000, as the VP of International Marketing for USANA Health Sciences, I was asked to develop a strategy that would return the company to growth and provide it with a foundation for steady growth. After some iteration and with the continuation of a methodical international expansion, the strategy we came up with was a success. USANA's stock eventually rebounded from a low of 30 cents a share (55 cents a share on December 4, 2000) to $17.75 per share on December 8, 2003 and has continued to perform. If you studied the revenue chart included in Chapter 7, you'll see that USANA is the only company that has seen steady income growth since that strategy was put in place beginning in mid-2000. What we learned and implemented at USANA can continue to serve as a blueprint for creating shareholder value in direct selling companies today.

Value Matters: To Customers and Distributors

We began our strategic planning effort by studying our competition and made two conclusions: 1) our products were elite among our competitors, and 2) the price was outside the range that customers were paying for competitive products. We made a strategic decision to target the 75% quartile in price. Our pricing philosophy was simple: formulate and position our products as the best products that deserved premium pricing and leave value on the table for consumers by backing off the premium position but well above the average price. We were the first direct selling company I'm aware of that repriced its product line to deliver customer value. The price of our leading multivitamin and mineral product, "The Essentials", was reduced from more than $53 to approximately $35. Customers loved our new pricing and distributors were emboldened to share the products more often without tying them to the business because they felt like the products were a great value.

USANA's chairman, Myron Wentz, described the initiative thusly in the company's 2000 Annual Report:

"Early in the year we took a single, bold step that will significantly shape the future of USANA; we implemented the Value Initiative, a pricing structure that makes our products considerably more affordable for consumers. This was an important component in the creation of what we refer to as the "Consumer-Approved Network Marketing" model. We believe that we are the first network marketing company to offer such a business model. While most network marketing companies service almost exclusively distributors who are also paid to sell the products, USANA's

customer base is now almost evenly divided between pure consumers (Preferred Customers) and Associates. We believe that our ability to attract consumers validates the quality of USANA's products and provides the true residual business income our Associates seek."

Sales stabilized after the launch of our Value Initiative, but we quickly learned that our decision to lower prices and increase margins at the expense of our distributors was slowing distributor enrollments. Because distributors earned less on the sale of each item, they had to sell more (or personally purchase and consume more) product to meet their minimum sales requirements. We realized that we had delivered consumer value but had ignored distributor value. We recognized that for the average distributor, the key measure of value was not calculated in consumer terms, but rather they were measuring the cost to remain active. We solved their value problem by reformulating and introducing a new product pack that was then priced to reduce the cost for distributors to remain active.

It took us an iteration, but when we finalized pricing that delivered on customer and distributor expectations—and both realized value in the way they measured it—the company began to see both top line and enrollment growth.

Investors can help their direct selling portfolio companies by pushing them to be more rigorous in measuring and responding to their customers' and distributors' perceptions of value.

Distributors Need Customers

The statement that distributors need customers is so basic that you may find it insulting to your intelligence, but believe it or not, many network marketing companies have built a business with almost no customers. In these companies, everyone is a distributor. This was the case in the early days at USANA, but nearly a decade before the channel turned its attention to this issue, we had identified the need to grow a strong and vibrant customer platform and started one of the channel's first preferred customer programs, beginning in earnest in 2000.

In December 2012, Bill Ackman of Pershing Square Capital began a short campaign against the stock of Herbalife. Ackman's campaign was very public and very critical of Herbalife's business model, claiming that it was a pyramid scheme. The intense public scrutiny and Ackman's public demand for an inquiry resulted in an FTC investigation of the company that concluded with a negotiated settlement, a fine and Herbalife's agreement to change some business practices and to submit to ongoing regulator audits. In February 2018, Ackman ended his public assault and admitted he had "unwound" his short positions in Herbalife.[39]

The intense scrutiny of direct selling that came about as a result of Ackman's attack on Herbalife has changed the dynamics of our channel for the better. Every major company has been focusing on customer value and has tried to uncouple the age-old practice of creating incentives for all customers to be distributors. Yes, that's right—companies actually

[39]   https://www.cnbc.com/2018/02/28/ackman-exits-bet-against-herbalife.html, accessed June 15, 2019.

created incentives for all customers to enroll as distributors and therefore most legacy companies have distributors who enrolled with no intention of selling, but rather just to get the distributor benefits. Let me explain …

Distinguishing Customers from Distributors

Traditionally, large network marketing companies were built almost exclusively on a personal consumption model. Or, said another way, distributors were not expected to actually sell or distribute the product to customers, but rather to use the product themselves and find other "distributors" who also wanted to use the product for themselves.

Legacy companies created incentives for everyone who wanted the product, business builders or true consumers, to join as distributors because the barrier to becoming a distributor was so low and the company significantly discounted the product's price for those who signed a distributor agreement. A few of these "customer distributors" became distributors that actually grew a business as a result of telling others about the success they had with the products. These few customer-to-distributor success stories convinced company executives and other distributors that this practice of encouraging every customer to become a distributor held promise as a recruitment tool. While these companies continued to offer a retail price and a wholesale price and allowed distributors to earn a commission on the difference between those two prices, the real compensation system and economic model assumed that all sales were made at the wholesale price.

Until the changes in thinking driven by the Ackman attack on Herbalife beginning in 2012, even though network marketers had retail pricing for customers, I estimate that most of all sales were made to distributors. This number was high not because companies didn't have anyone but distributors who wanted their products, but because their pricing incentives were such that it didn't make sense NOT to be a distributor.

Once a customer became a distributor, they were subject to the same monthly minimum production requirements to maintain the discount that was offered to distributors who were producing monthly sales. In other words, they had to place personal orders every month to keep their distributor discount active. These monthly minimums had been put in place to help companies create some distinction between a customer who had to purchase at a retail price and the distributors who could purchase at wholesale prices. Because companies understood that most of their distributors were customers, they set these monthly minimums relatively low, typically at an amount that would represent 100% loyalty to the product(s) being sold and 100% compliance for a one-month period. As long as a customer/distributor used their product(s) every day, they could consume all of the product they were buying every month to meet the monthly minimums and could continue receiving the discounted price.

Today's autoship programs began as "backup orders." If those with a distributor agreement failed to meet their monthly minimum, rather than lose their status and lose their discount, they would designate a "backup order" that would be triggered on the last week of the month to preserve their qualification status. The autoship programs, then, were built not to support a customer's actual consumption pattern, but to support distributors' monthly minimum production requirements and to make sure the distributors did not become disqualified. These minimums also helped maintain stable earnings for distributors because the sales incentives were often built on the number of "active" distributors on a sales team. The customers win because they receive a lower price, the true distributors win because they meet their organization sales requirements, and the company wins with steady and growing sales.

The channel as a whole has seen the need to separate customers from distributors mostly because of the economic value of doing so, but also because some companies fear the regulatory risk of not changing. However, many legacy direct sellers are still plagued by the technology and incentive systems originally built to support the "customers are our distributors" model. As the channel has evolved in separating customers from distributors, so too have the channel's learning and strategies improved.

As an investor, you will want to understand where a company is on the spectrum of "customers are our distributors" as opposed to "our distributors sell to customers." Many companies can use more retail marketing expertise to help them formulate plans to improve the value of their customers. Buyer beware if the company you are considering continues to give little thought to acquiring and selling to non-distributor customers.

New Products or Product Categories

Amway has been a trailblazer in direct selling for many years. In the early 90s when I first joined Melaleuca, Inc., Amway clearly considered itself a distribution channel and as such tested almost every imaginable product and service. Other companies recognizing the quantity of distributors and customers who were loyal to direct sellers would approach companies to offer credit cards, phone service, travel and other discount programs for sale through their distributors. These experiments lasted for just a few years and companies began to realize that while their distributors wanted new products, they couldn't effectively sell (or often wouldn't buy) products and services they didn't see as a core competency of the company. The idea of direct selling as a product distributor is evolving to recognize direct selling companies as brands and their distributors as extensions of their brand. The basic rules of brand extension must be applied in their strictest form within the channel. Introducing new products that are off-brand into a company doesn't work but introducing new and/or improved products can create value.

When I first arrived at USANA, the company was following the channel norm of relying on quarterly events and new product launches at those events to drive excitement and growth. It didn't take long for me to realize that the company's product line was expanding faster than our revenue line. New product plans always predicted incremental sales, but rarely produced any noticeable change in average order size or frequency. What we learned at USANA and what has since become more widely known among consumable product companies is that new products do not lead to more sales, only increased costs. (Note: this is not true in fashion, jewelry, fragrances and most party plan or demonstration sales products. New products do lead to more sales, but these companies would be wise to create a method of retiring products on a regular basis).

We began to experiment with "news" other than new products, and found that an announcement of a partnership, sponsorship or new program was as motivating as a new product. We applied our value learnings and began to reformulate products rather than creating new ones. We also combined a few products, delivering great value to our consumers and distributors and significant profit improvements for the company.

It wasn't until my tenure as the head of Beachbody's network marketing company that I would fully appreciate the last important part of a new product plan: the cadence or timing of new product introductions. When I arrived at Beachbody, they had planned new product launches around seasonal interest in weight loss, adjusted slightly to account for television inventory (the company's primary revenues came from its infomercial business at the time). As the growth of the network marketing division accelerated and it became clear that it would be our future, we rethought the cadence and came up with a predictable pattern of product launches and promotions. The predictability and pattern created operational efficiencies in the company, but its real impact came in the field as our part-time sellers learned how to prepare and maximize each promotion and new product. Our growth continued to accelerate.

Given the combined experiences I have had, I have also come to realize how important it is to consider a new product in light of a company's selling system, which I described in more detail in Chapter 4. For example, Avon used a simple system for years—deliver consumers a printed catalog and rely on the catalog to sell. As long as a new product can be sold on the pages of a catalog, it fits the system.

If I were running a direct selling company today, I would review every new product proposal to first determine if the product is revolutionary or evolutionary. Evolutionary product can be slotted into the product plan with clear instruction on how it complements the current selling system, which should be built around a hero product. If a product has the potential of becoming a new hero, I would task the sales team to not only focus innovation around the product, but also around the system for selling it. I would never launch a potential hero without launching it with a clear and tested system for selling it. In my opinion, great direct sellers don't sell. *They execute a system and the system sells.*

Investors can help create value in companies that lack a sound product strategy, a thoughtful new product introduction cadence, or a long-term product pipeline. For direct selling companies, a "thoughtful" product strategy means that proper consideration has been given to the current selling system and how new products will fit into it. Product strategy is particularly important to those companies that do not have a consumable product. For example, fashion, home decor, kitchen tools and home furnishing companies all live and die on the quality of their new products and the soundness of thinking around frequency, launch communication, pricing and positioning.

Retention and Reactivation

While at USANA, I led several efforts to improve retention and learned two important lessons: 1) retention is rarely transactional, but instead is an outcome of properly executed processes and systems; and 2) reactivation is a marketer's mirage that looks so appealing, but the math just doesn't add up.

As head of marketing, I was asked to work with our customer service department to test save campaigns, loyalty programs and other incentives to try and increase the number of orders we received from our customers and distributors. Few of these programs showed meaningful results. By the time customers called to place an order, they seemed determined to stop future orders from coming and we couldn't seem to change their minds.

During the strategic planning process, I referenced earlier, I commissioned several focus groups with distributors/customers we had defined as being canceled. The company's definition of active or canceled was based on our technology capability. Either you had an active autoship or had ordered manually last month and were therefore "active" or you hadn't, and you were defined as "canceled." We invited those who had not purchased recently to tell us why they were no longer customers.

Through these focus groups, we were shocked to learn that many of the "canceled" individuals were still consuming USANA's products. They loved the products and considered themselves loyal users, but because they were inconsistent in taking them, they had canceled their account so they could catch up and consume all the products we had sent them during the months they were involved. In other words, our "retention problem" was in part a function of our program's design and the technology that supported our program. These customers didn't want to end their relationship with us, they just wanted to pause it, and we didn't have a mechanism for offering that option. We had not built our IT systems around the consumer experience, but rather around our compensation plan and software capabilities.

At the time, the easy way to increase retention was to simply align our definition with our customer's definition. However, this would have required that our order entry system be fixed to allow these individuals to control the frequency of their orders. Believe it or not, that seemed impossible given the IT systems supporting the business at the time, and the mindset we had toward using a subscription service to power the compensation program. But the learning from these focus groups changed the way I looked at retention. Instead of offering a deal to get someone to place one more order, I learned how important it was to first focus on the customer experience. Retention becomes a natural result when you design your product and customer experience to more perfectly match the customer's needs and expectations. Good design increases retention. Tactical transaction level incentives don't.

While direct selling companies can make improvements in retention, the channel tends to have characteristically high turnover rates. Jim Northrop, CEO of Winfield Consulting, believes that many investors analyze a company and draw the wrong conclusions about its sustainability with such high turnover. In our interview, Northrop said that too many investors conclude that direct selling is unstable because there are so many people leaving all the time.

"What these investors fail to understand," Northrop said, "is that it's a fundamentally dynamic model where people come in, they develop—some of them—they mature, and they tend to age out. Your entire model is predicated on your ability to continually refresh your gene pool, continually developing new people to be new leaders."

According to one leading direct selling consultant, 50% of new distributors last less than three months. In their book **Launch Smart: How to Build a Direct Sales Company**, consultants and authors Terrel Transtrum and Craig Fleming write that "… 80% attrition in the first year is the average for network marketing companies, and 60% is the average for party plan companies." Transtrum and Fleming site four substantiating studies for their statistics conducted by ServiceQuest, the Direct Selling Association, *HARVARD BUSINESS REVIEW* and Wirthlin.

Transtrum and Fleming go on to argue that direct selling companies can improve their retention and can experience significant financial gains for doing so. They write: "A study published by the Boston based firm of Bain and Company concludes that a 5% improvement in retention can result in as much as 25 to 95% increase in profits. Moreover, a mere 2% improvement in retention is the equivalent to a 10% reduction in expenses."

Even with statistics showing opportunities to significantly improve retention, many executives have been slow to focus on retention efforts. Why? In part because the model does not have the speculative marketing expenses of other channels. Direct selling companies only pay for results, not for the prospects of results. Said another way, retention and/or reactivation programs often require the company to put capital at risk and incur an expense in the hope that there will be a result but recruiting new distributors and new customers is a risk-free, pay-only-for-results program. Given the choice, they ignore retention and focus on recruiting new customers and distributors.

Successful direct selling executives don't ignore retention but have learned the difference between programs designed to retain versus those trying to rescue or revive.   Transtrum said that time spent on improving retention before someone cancels has a very high ROI, but once someone cancels, there is little evidence that time and programs produce a return. To illustrate his point, he told me about an experience early in his career at Melaleuca, Inc.

"We sent out 300,000 mailers inviting all of the people that had been on our autoship program at one time to come back," he said. "We offered them free products with some really good reasons to come back. Out of three hundred thousand, we had eight hundred sign back up and I think we had like fifty out of those stay on for a month after they got their free product."

Many executives have confused retention with rescue programs and concluded that retention isn't important. Instead of spending time on programs to fix retention, they have in fact found it easier to recruit new customers and new distributors. In contrast, executives from leading companies track retention. These executives understand that it may not be possible to see a massive departure from the average, but they know that a small improvement in retention can produce a significant improvement in profitability.   Great companies focus on making small incremental improvements in customer service, product effectiveness, and consumer convenience. They also employ and train a focused "save team" in their call center and give them the tools necessary to respond to the customer's needs and desires. In other words, knowing what to do and at what stage of the customer experience to apply retention efforts is the key to success.

Great companies devote some resources to improved retention and make modifications in training, communication, product and community that improve stickiness. Most of the changes companies can and should make not only impact retention but also will accelerate customer and distributor acquisition. For example, when we invited Beachbody's customers to join with other customers to hold each other accountable to a workout program, we found that those who participated were more likely to have success, more likely to remain active at least through the completion of the program, and more likely to become distributors themselves. Companies that reward distributors not just for recruiting new customers but also for retaining those customers longer found improved retention, and because distributors were earning more and being recognized for that additional activity, the distributor retention rate increased as well.

Now a few words of warning to investors and new advisors: *Be thoughtful about the arguments you use to encourage a focus on retention and the weight you give to retention.*

Some investors try to make the argument that a company will someday "run out" of customers or potential distributors, but this is a problem most executives would love to be challenged with. Even with several companies with decades of sales and billions in revenues, the channel as a whole has penetrated less than 17% of U.S. households and accounts for less than 1% of U.S. retail sales. No company in the channel has yet been fortunate enough to have to worry about "getting to the end of the row."

Investors and board members should be careful not to divert to much attention to retention activities. Companies that turn their resources from finding and recruiting "new"—even if their new focus is on saving the existing—almost always have found that both numbers decline. New customers and distributors are the lifeblood of direct selling and should always be treated as such.

Great direct sellers have found the right balance between retention and recruiting and have learned to avoid spending too much effort on reactivation. Too many direct selling executives fail to focus on retention or on the right levers that can impact retention, and investors can be helpful in redirecting their efforts without taking the company's eye off the primary driver of new customer and distributor acquisition or recruiting.

Technology Refresh

Another important part of the work we did at USANA was the company's investment in technology. As the company began to expand to additional international markets, it began to realize how limited they were by the current direct selling software they were using to calculate commissions, take orders, run operations and provide management and distributors with data. They invested heavily in technology and built their own software system, which they titled *Odyssey*.

For more than a decade I have attended gatherings of the top CEOs in direct selling and almost without exception, those meetings have always included time spent talking about the inadequacy of the technology systems available in the channel. The channel's complex compensation systems have created such a unique stratum between a transaction and data and operating layers, it has been very difficult for companies to use off-the-shelf specialty software (Salesforce, Shopify, Magento, etc.), and therefore most can benefit from a focused review and refresh of their technology.

Today's direct sellers are often struggling with mobile technology, data warehousing and reporting, and almost all are woefully behind other industries when it comes to ecommerce and follow-on remarketing and email marketing. Experienced and connected investors can create significant value by helping get non-channel technology expertise involved to accelerate the company's technology modernization.

International Expansion

I've met some CEOs who have been hesitant to expand internationally. These executives typically argue that they have barely tapped their U.S. market potential ... why would they want to aim their limited time and resources elsewhere? It is hard to argue that most direct sellers don't have upside opportunity in the U.S. It's also true that there are changes happening in the U.S. economy that could alter the dynamics of success for U.S. direct sellers in the future. But it is crucial for investors to understand one fact: NO direct selling company has reached and sustained a billion dollars in sales in the United States alone. Even some of the largest companies have found it difficult to sustain $500 million in sales over a long period of time. If you choose to bet on a U.S.-

only strategy, realize that you are plowing new ground and you risk losing momentum if your company is growing with sales north of $600 million.

During my tenure at USANA, we had one of the channel's most successful international executives, Bradford Richardson, at the helm. Under his leadership, I played only a supporting role in international expansion, but from his success at USANA and later at Shaklee, I learned how valuable international expansion can be to a direct selling company. As valuable as our strategies were in creating a foundation for USANA and in renewing the distributors' belief in the company, had we not started on the path of global expansion we would have not experienced the long-term growth I referenced above. International expansion is a key component to long-term growth in direct selling and often companies err in being too aggressive or too slow to pursue international growth.

For direct selling companies, the cost of international expansion is typically much less than the cost for brick-and-mortar retailers, and marginally more than the cost of continuing in a single market. In 2017 (the most recent data reported) global direct sales totaled $189 billion with approximately 18% ($34.9 billion) coming from the U.S. Many of the largest direct selling companies mimic these global statistics and report more than 80% of their sales outside the U.S. Given these statistics, the opportunity for geographic expansion is real, but it is also true that most companies with international operations have multiple countries losing money. Here is what I learned from watching Richardson and from studying the successful expansion of other companies like Nu Skin:

Make sure you have field leaders with contacts and who have a willingness to go and build their business in the market(s) you intend to open. (NOTE: It's better to start with a smaller market where you have leaders ready to help you than to focus on a large opportunity without field support). While data showing the popularity of your product category in a country is directional and helpful, it pales in comparison to your leaders' relationships and/or willingness to build in a market.

Invest in hiring experienced management with international experience and with experience in a particular country or region you plan to open.

Don't rush it. Make sure the company has a plan with plenty of time built in for required product registration and licensing (this can take months or more than a year depending on the market).

Where should you go if you're thinking about international expansion? The short answer is "wherever your leaders have the best contacts and a willingness to travel and build." The data would say that while there are a few (mostly local) direct sellers who have had success in Europe or South America, most international success still comes from Asia. If you don't have leaders with a desire to expand and grow their business internationally, often you can find these leaders in Canada or Australia. Both of these countries have traditionally been places where you can enroll distributors with more international experience and contacts, and though small in number, they can be strategically important. Mexico, though large, has been a mixed market for many and the United Kingdom has been both a disaster and a bonanza depending on the company and the in-country management.

In addition to the strategies that we found successful at USANA, there are others you may consider that can increase shareholder value, and others that you might wish to avoid based on my observations and experience.

U.S. Geographic Expansion

I recently was asked to join a company's strategic planning process and to partner with one of the world's leading strategy consulting firms to prepare a five-year strategic plan for a large U.S.-based direct selling company. As you would expect, the consulting firm went through an extensive evaluation and data analysis before they came back with five strategic recommendations. According to their report, the recommendation with the most economic upside was a campaign to focus on white space opportunities in the United States as the company prepared for international expansion. In other words, they showed how the company had grown in a few key states in the South and Midwest and showed that capturing a similar "fair share" of category sales in other states would more than double sales.

From a theoretical perspective, attacking U.S. white space sounds simple, but from a practical standpoint, I have yet to find a direct selling company that has proven an ability to target geographic expansion within the United States. Even when the white space is language-based (i.e. U.S. Spanish), there is a mixed success rate. Geographic targeting, like deciding to grow California, for example, is a strategy waiting for a success story.

It is possible that direct selling companies have not been willing to invest capital in traditional media and that a decision to do so could be key to expanding geographically in the U.S. I hope the channel can figure out how to crack this code as I believe it has so much to offer to urban America and to lower-income neighborhoods. If you decide that you are going to invest and help lead a portfolio company to success in capturing new U.S. white space, make sure you have a channel expert review the plan before you invest to help you avoid failures of the past. If you're going into an investment believing that greenfield expansion in the U.S. is the ticket to restarting growth in a company without momentum, know that you are laying track in a yet untapped wilderness of opportunity.

New Channels of Distribution

Beachbody is the one direct selling company with a history of success in employing multiple channels to sell their products. Some may argue that Rodan + Fields has also been successful in multiple channels, but technically it was never a multi-channel business. According to Lori Bush, former CEO of Rodan + Fields, "Proactiv, the DTC acne product marketed by Guthy Renker, was kept completely separate and there was no cross-over other than to refer to the doctors as the creators of Proactiv."

I believe Beachbody's success and Rodan + Field's ability to build a successful direct selling business despite having similar products in another channel was due to the fact that they started as direct marketing (infomercial) businesses and expanded into direct selling. Beachbody was successful in convincing distributors that they were building brands and generating demand with their TV sales (direct response and QVC). Even with the benefit of TV-built brands, Beachbody was forced to create a hero product that was exclusively sold by its direct selling division in order to make the multi-channel strategy work.

Aside from Beachbody, Avon, Tupperware and a few others have attempted alternative channel strategies and abandoned those efforts relatively soon after launch. Direct sellers view other channels as a direct affront and a sign that a company is "not committed" to the distributors and is, in fact, attempting to eliminate them in the future. At least one private equity-funded company has seen more than $200 million in revenue disappear almost immediately after the new CEO expressed interest in moving into new channels of distribution. If your strategy is to take a direct selling company's product into a new channel, understand that the decision could cost you all or most of your direct selling revenue. If you aren't prepared to take that risk then before you proceed you need to find a way to convince your field that it is in their best interest for you to be in another channel and show them how that decision will benefit them.

New Management

Direct selling has traditionally found it difficult to compete for talent and often is led by management with very little large company experience. It is accurate, therefore, to believe that improving a management team could create value. In making a change, be sure to:

Hire CEOs, presidents, lawyers and sales VPs with direct selling experience. Because there are so many subtle yet critical nuances in this channel, leaders without experience can make costly mistakes. Nu Skin CEO Ritch Wood warned: "So often a private equity firm will bring in a high-level executive from the beauty or retail space who doesn't understand direct selling. Before you know it, the decisions that are being made are not in favor of the sales force which is your most critical asset. At the end of the day, the business starts to struggle, or all the decisions are made around the bottom line and whenever decisions are made not in favor of the sales force it tends to create problems over time. Whoever is asked to manage the business really has to know the space." Avon has struggled for many years and some say their downfall began when they started to hire leadership from outside the channel. However, Herbalife hired Michael Johnson as CEO and after a year or so of what he described as painful learning; Johnson's tenure has been a noteworthy exception to this recommendation.

Take your time. "The most significant dynamic that investors tend to misunderstand, or underestimate is the importance of the founders," said MidOcean Partners' Eric Roth. "Investors typically want to assemble a fully professionalized management team, which should be done incrementally and with caution lest you compromise the company DNA that made it successful in the first place."

Make sure your transition plan includes the appropriate face-to-face communication with field leaders. When replacing leaders who have been field facing, always assume the field's first reaction will be to support the leader, not the company. The good news is that most new management can win over the field with plenty of effort made to communicate with them and a deliberate plan to build relationships early.

One last warning regarding management changes. Often investors respond to declining sales after a transaction closes by replacing management. Darren Jensen, CEO of LifeVantage, warns that investors often don't understand the cycles of direct selling.

"After the momentum begins to slow or even decline after a growth phase," Jensen explained, "an investor group may come in and say, 'Well, I have ineffective management here. Let's wipe them out and bring in other people.' Or they may say 'we need to change the compensation plan.' They don't understand that doing either of these will paralyze the entire distributor base and make it harder to return to growth. They have injected additional uncertainty and have just sped the descent because they took away the existing relationships that could have possibly changed the trajectory of the declining sales."

Operational Efficiencies

Many direct selling companies will benefit from investors who can bring experienced operational know how to the company. Almost any type of improvement is conceivable, with the possible exception of turning a manufacturer into a contract manufacturer. It is almost impossible to keep secrets from the field and if they think the company is attempting to sell the same product under a different brand, the field's trust in the company will take a hit and make it more difficult for the company to keep distributors during tough times. While it would be difficult for a company to contract manufacture for others, companies can and do hire third party manufacturers and distribution partners to help them improve their quality and service levels.

Now that we've reviewed some of the nuances of the channel when it comes to employing strategic improvements, it's time to talk more about how the channel's uniqueness should impact your consideration of transactions that will help you realize value.

Chapter 10

Creating Value Via Transactions

At the end of November 2018, *Barron's* reported this stunning fact: "Private-equity firms amassed $1.14 trillion in uninvested capital—or dry powder—by the end of September, according to data provider Preqin."[40] With that amount of cash looking for a return, it only makes sense that private equity professionals not only seek out opportunities to accelerate returns with operational improvements, but also explore ways to efficiently deploy more capital to improve returns. In this chapter, we will first look at how capital might be deployed to improve returns via M&A, and then we'll consider transactions that will create returns before and at an exit.

Mergers and Acquisitions

The mainstream opinion of most of the CEOs I interviewed is that trying to combine two direct selling sales forces to make a full merger of two companies is difficult if not impossible. There are few examples of

---

[40]   https://www.barrons.com/articles/5-signs-were-in-a-private-equity-bubble-1543514770, accessed May 29, 2019.

success. However, as you will read in the appendix in my review of the publicized (and some not so publicized) deals that have been done in the channel's history, there have been plenty of attempts despite the common belief that mergers are not wise.

Almost every CEO I interviewed claimed that they had looked at acquisitions, but those who actually followed through with a transaction opted only to acquire manufacturers, companies that gave them access to strategic markets like China, or companies that expanded other vertical capabilities. Asked why they hadn't acquired other direct selling companies, the CEOs almost always pointed to culture and compensation plan and argued that it was almost impossible to effectively mix cultures and compensation plans.

"Companies come to us all the time wanting us to acquire them" said Isagenix CEO Travis Ogden. "And so far, today, we've said no to all of them. That's not to say that there won't be one that makes sense in the future. The hardest thing, from my perspective, and the reason why it doesn't make a lot of sense is because of the compensation plans. Merging compensation plans is cumbersome and difficult."

Despite the difficulty, there are examples of direct selling companies that have acquired other direct selling companies. In fact, I led the acquisition of a direct selling company as part of my role as CEO of Origami Owl. We acquired a small skin care company named willa because we had similar cultures (they had also been started by a mother and daughter), similar target customers, and similar compensation plans. Our strategy was to hedge our fashion jewelry product line that was showing signs of "perceived saturation" (though no real evidence of true saturation) with a consumable line of skincare products. We saw triple digit growth in the company we acquired during the first year but found that having two companies within one entity created confusion and increased stress among our top leaders. While our experience doesn't make me rule out an acquisition, I would probably not recommend a similar strategy to others in the future.

It appears that there are two types of successful acquisitions: 1) a large company acquiring a much smaller company and merging products and distributors into their current compensation system, and 2) companies being acquired and left as independent entities like *Nature's Sunshine acquisition of Synergy*. Nature's Sunshine was known for having an aging salesforce. Synergy has continued as a separate brand and has brought the company young distributors and a hope for renewal in the future.

With the exception of the deals I've listed below, most of the acquisitions I have been able to identify were characterized by a large company purchasing small or failing companies in deals that likely included little capital.   The following are a few of the mergers that have taken place.

Traditional Acquisitions with Integration

Modere and Jusuru: One of the most successful acquisitions and integrations was Modere's acquisition of Jusuru. Not only did Modere receive some much-needed salesforce strength in the U.S., but they also effectively launched Jusuru's products. The big win for shareholders was in the leadership that Jusuru brought. Jusuru's founder and CEO Asma

Ishaq eventually became the CEO of Modere and has led an impressive reinvigoration of the company.

Thirty-One Gifts and Jewel Kade: Thirty-One Gifts purchased Jewel Kade's jewelry line and distributors. In the end it launched only a few pieces under the Jewel Kade by Thirty-One brand and had success bringing over several (but certainly not all) of Jewel Kade's leading distributors.

Young Living Essential Oils and Life Matters: Life Matters was acquired in 2017 in a non-cash deal. Life Matters' well-known founder and CEO Richard Brookes came in the deal and Young Living integrated Life Matters' products into their line.[41]   Brookes told me that the unusually strong retention numbers Young Living had been able to achieve over decades in business were enough to convince him that he and his distributors would be better off joining the larger company. The management of Young Living agreed.

Zija International and XANGO: When Zija International acquired XANGO, the press release read, "The acquisition was made possible through the efforts of Zija's Founder Ken Brailsford, who also co-founded Nature's Sunshine and founded Enrich International (now Unicity). 'Every one of the XANGO founders has worked with Ken during our careers,' said XANGO Founder, CEO and Chairman Aaron Garrity. 'Ken brought my partner Joe and I into the direct selling business and shaped the early parts of our careers. He is a mentor and a trusted friend. Ken has always shown deep respect for what we have all built with XANGO, and he

---

[41]   https://www.directsellingnews.com/young-living-acquires-nutrition-company-life-matters/, accessed May 29, 2019.

shares our belief that a company in our industry must make distributors its top priority.'"[42]

Vertical Integration

In search of an effective way to deploy capital, a few companies have started to aggressively pursue acquisitions to capture more value in the supply chain. Bouncer Schiro, Chairman and CEO of energy giant Stream Energy, acknowledged the challenge of efficiently deploying capital.

"I would think that if you become a manufacturer and go vertical with your stack it gives you an opportunity to be a little more profitable," he said.

A few companies that have made vertical acquisitions are:

Nu Skin

R&D/Intellectual Property

2011—acquired genomics company LifeGen Technologies for $12 million. Acquisition included LifeGen's collection of patents and technology.[43]

2012—acquired NOX Technologies, Inc., a biotechnology and bio diagnostic company based in Malvern, Pennsylvania for $12.5 million. The agreement included the acquisition of technology and patents, including previously licensed technology already utilized in connection with Nu Skin's anti-aging research efforts.[44]

---

[42]   https://www.directsellingnews.com/zija-international-acquires-xango/, accessed May 29, 2019.
[43] http://www.lsbmn.org/2011/12/nu-skin-acquires-lifegen/, accessed May 29, 2019.

Manufacturing

2018—Nu Skin announced that they had "acquired three companies that, respectively, manufacture products for the personal care and nutrition industries and specialize in product packaging. These companies provide products and services not only to our core Nu Skin business but also to external customers so that these companies can build their own brands within their own industries to better achieve their growth potential. Our manufacturing and packaging companies generated $90.6 million of our 2018 reported revenue (excluding sales to our core Nu Skin business)."[45]

Wasatch Product Development (a.k.a. Wasatch Labs and formerly owned by USANA) – personal care products.

Elevate Health Sciences – nutrition products

CasePak- packaging

USANA Health Sciences

Media and Events

2004—acquired FMG Productions to produce live events and video content (FMG Productions founder Kevin Guest is now USANA's CEO).

---

[44] https://www.prnewswire.com/news-releases/nu-skin-enterprises-enters-into-agreement-to-acquire-nox-technologies-179267281.html, accessed May 29, 2019.

[45] https://www.marketwatch.com/press-release/10-k-nu-skin-enterprises-inc-2019-02-14, accessed May 29, 2019.

Manufacturing

2003—acquired Wasatch Product Development, Inc. to manufacture skin and personal care products[46] NOTE: Wasatch Product Development is now owned by Nu Skin.

Amway

Manufacturing

1960—purchased a 50% share in Atco Manufacturing Company in Detroit, the original manufacturers of LOC, and changed its name to Amway Manufacturing Corporation.

Herbalife

Manufacturing

2009—Herbalife Ltd. (NYSE: HLF), acquired Micelle Laboratories, a contract manufacturer of food and nutritional supplements in the powder, liquid, tablet and capsule delivery forms, in order to strengthen its global manufacturing capabilities.[47]

Technology/R&D

2011—acquired iChange, a nutrition and health network and former Vator Splash finalist. Terms of the deal were not disclosed.[48]

2017—formed a joint venture with Tasly Holding Group, which focuses on developing Traditional Chinese Medicine-based products. The

---

[46] https://www.sec.gov/Archives/edgar/data/896264/0001157523-03-002923.txt, accessed May 29, 2019.

[47] https://ir.herbalife.com/news-releases/news-release-details/herbalife-acquires-us-manufacturing-facility, accessed May 29, 2019.

[48] https://vator.tv/news/2011-04-24-ichange-a-healthy-acquisition-for-herbalife, accessed May 29, 2019.

JV is aimed at developing and commercializing novel health products, benefiting from Tasly's scientific know-how.[49]

Market America

2010- acquired Shop.com with the stated purpose of harnessing the power of technology to provide a high touch, personal shopping experience combined with the depth of selection available through instant search of the more than 43 million products in our database.[50]

Acquiring for International Expansion

China is one of the most dynamic markets for direct sellers and should be a cornerstone of any company's international expansion plans. Bradford Richardson, the former president of Shaklee International and one of the channel's most successful international executives, believes that having at least a blueprint for China is key.

"Even if you don't plan on going to China immediately, you have to have a China strategy before you launch operations in any other country," he said. "Sooner or later your international leaders will be asking you about your China strategy."

---

[49] https://ir.herbalife.com/news-releases/news-release-details/herbalife-nutrition-and-tasly-holding-group-form-ht-innovations, accessed June 15, 2019.

[50] https://www.prnewswire.com/news-releases/market-america-to-acquire-shopcom-business-to-create-social-shopping-site-positioned-to-rival-internets-leading-shopping-destinations-111919989.html, accessed June 26, 2019.

China has been a very successful market for the large direct sellers who entered the market early. Unfortunately, the government has slowed almost to a stop the issuing of new direct selling licenses, making the country a significant challenge to companies not doing business there now. Some companies have found it critical to have Chinese partners to help them navigate the politics and cultural nuances there. In the past two decades, a few companies have made acquisitions or entered into mergers to assist them in their China business. Here are a few examples of these M&A deals:

2010—USANA Health Sciences, Inc. (NASDAQ: USNA) acquired BabyCare Ltd, a China-based direct selling company. In the press release announcing the deal, Dave Wentz, then USANA's chief executive officer, said, "We are very excited about this acquisition and the opportunity that it provides for USANA to ultimately establish a business via BabyCare in China. BabyCare is a natural fit for us, as they share our philosophy for high-quality products and pristine manufacturing practices. In fact, 15 of BabyCare's nutritional supplement products are qualified by SFDA, the Government's highest level of product regulatory approval. As a company with over 11 years of in-country experience, and as one of only 25 companies operating with a direct selling license in China, BabyCare brings us both valuable knowledge of China's direct selling market and the ability to expand our business in China via BabyCare. We believe this acquisition is the most effective way for us to enter this enormous market."[51]

2014—Nature's Sunshine Products, Inc. (NASDAQ: NATR), created a joint venture with Shanghai Fosun Pharmaceutical (Group) Co., Ltd. ("Fosun Pharma"; stock code: 600196-SH 2196.HK) to market and distribute Nature's Sunshine and Synergy products in China.

2017—Xyngular acquired Symmetry Global. The acquisition was essentially the combination of companies gave Xyngular a presence in the Philippines and the Caribbean market through an already established company. It was expected that Symmetry distributors would become part of Xyngular's salesforce.[52]

Acquiring New Brands and Products

Historically, a few companies have successfully purchased companies with the express purpose of folding the acquired company's products into their existing distribution channel. One notable acquisition was Nu Skin's acquisition of retail nutritional supplement brand Pharmanex in 1988. Nu Skin initially built a separate compensation system and offered Pharmanex as a business separate from its skin care business sold under the Nu Skin brand. Eventually, the company scrapped the two- brand strategy (actually three brands, since they had

---

[51]   https://www.businesswire.com/news/home/20100816006649/en/USANA-Health-Sciences-Acquires-BabyCare-Direct-Selling, accessed May 29, 2019.
[52]   https://www.directsellingnews.com/xyngular-acquires-symmetry-global/, accessed June 15, 2019.

also launched Big Planet to offer internet services) and folded Pharmanex successfully into the Nu Skin product offering.

When direct selling companies acquire brands/products to sell, they almost always do so with the intent to discontinue the sale of these products/brands in any other channel. In an article announcing the acquisition of Pharmanex by Nu Skin, Deseret News staff writer Dennis Romboy said that Nu Skin planned to pull Pharmanex's products from "shelves at some 30,000 retail outlets like American Stores and Walmart." He quoted then Pharmanex president Bill McGlashan as saying, "This has never been done before ... (retailers) can't quite fathom why we would do this."

McGlashan then articulated two compelling benefits for taking this unconventional approach:

Ability to Tell the Product Story. McGlashan was quoted as saying, "I can have an army of distributors whom we can educate and train. If I had ten minutes to sit down and talk to you about Tegreen (a potent antioxidant Pharmanex sells), you'd be using Tegreen for life."

Selling Power of Nu Skin's Distributors. Romboy wrote: "The 34-year-old Pharmanex founder sees Nu Skin as a vehicle to even more than the $20 million in sales the company anticipates this year. McGlashan figures it will earn as much in several months with network marketing as it would during a year in stores."[53]

Here are a few product/brand acquisitions:

---

[53]   https://www.deseretnews.com/article/663549/Pharmanex-abandoning-retail-for-direct-selling.html, accessed May 29, 2019.

1998—Nu Skin acquired Generation Health, the parent company of the dietary supplement company Pharmanex.

1999—Nu Skin acquired Big Planet, an internet-based technology company that offers e-commerce and other technology services.[54]

1972—Amway acquired Nutrilite, a company the founders had represented and product the Amway distributors had sold previously.

2015—Amway acquired California-based energy drink brand XS Energy.

2018—Regal Ware Inc. acquired coffee and tea press company ESPRO[55]

M&A Portfolio Strategies

Since Y2K, several direct selling companies and a few investor groups have looked at making acquisitions as part of a portfolio strategy. These deals have been done with the intention of rolling together multiple brands with differing degrees of sales force integration. Some companies keep the acquired company autonomous in sales and marketing, leveraging operational efficiencies only. Other companies offer the sales organization the chance to sell any or all of the company's portfolio of products as it expands those offerings via acquisitions.

When asked if he thought there would be more publicly traded direct selling companies in the future, Nu Skin CEO Ritch Wood said he is

---

[54] https://www.chiefmarketer.com/nu-skin-to-acquire-big-planet/, accessed May 29, 2019.
[55] https://www.directsellingnews.com/regal-ware-inc-acquires-coffee-and-tea-press-company-espro/, accessed May 29, 2019.

intrigued by the possibility of a portfolio company being a strong strategic option in the future.

"I think the very best strategy would be a public enterprise that would put more than one direct seller on the same platform," he said. "... a conglomerate would be an amazing strategy."

There are several examples of companies pursuing a portfolio strategy. The most public failure was Avon's $650 million acquisition of Silpada (to be detailed in the appendix) which began to see sales decline immediately after the deal closed. Silpada was eventually sold back to the owners for pennies on the dollar. Other examples have been a bit more enduring.

JRJR Networks, formerly CVSL. JRJR Networks was a holding company of direct selling companies until it filed for Chapter 11 bankruptcy in 2018. JRJR Networks traded on the NYSE, before it was removed from the exchange due to lack of capitalization. The company had invested in several direct sellers including Agel, Betterware, Kleeneze, Longaberger, Paperly, Tomboy Tools, Uppercase Living, and Your Inspiration at Home, and was unable to make the strategy work. The firm tended to purchase companies in distress and allegedly had little capital to deploy to portfolio companies.

Blyth, Inc. (NYSE: BTH). Blyth acquired and held two direct selling companies: PartyLite and then Visalus. The company never completed the multi-stage purchase of Visalus because of falling revenues in that division and pulled out of the deal. It subsequently was acquired by the private equity firm Carlyle Group.

ARIIX. Ariix began as a nutritional supplement direct selling company but has eventually transformed itself into a portfolio of direct sellers purchased in the past few years including: Trivani in 2011, Voluxa in 2015, Asantae in 2016, NuCerity 2018 and ENVY Jewellery in 2018.

Total Life Changes (TLC). In 2016 Total Life Changes revealed plans to pursue a portfolio strategy and announced its first acquisition of Ryte, saying that it intended to acquire "smaller companies in need who share our ideals."[56]

Youngevity International, Inc. (NASDAQ: YGYI). Youngevity is the only publicly traded company that continues to pursue a pure portfolio strategy. The company has announced acquisitions of retail brands (that have not been required to give up sales in other channels) and of direct selling brands. Youngevity has traditionally looked for companies and brands that can be purchased with no or little cash. The structure of their deals and their integration plan was best captured in the press release announcing one of their biggest acquisitions—Beauticontrol from Tupperware. The press release said:

"Youngevity will integrate Beauticontrol's sales force into its company, marketing Beauticontrol branded products, as well as the other brands in Youngevity's extensive product portfolio. Youngevity will also market Beauticontrol branded products to its existing member base. Tupperware will earn a royalty based on future sales of the Beauticontrol sales force, and sales of the Beauticontrol product line by the existing Youngevity members.[57]

---

[56]   https://www.directsellingnews.com/total-life-changes-announces-first-acquisition/, accessed May 29, 2019.
[57]   https://www.prnewswire.com/news-releases/tupperware-brands-announces-

Youngevity's acquisitions have included Beauticontrol; Biometics; Botanical Spa Escape International; GOFoods;™ Healing America™ Heritage Makers; JavaFit® Livinity;™ Mineral Makeup Collection; ProJoba International;™ PureWorks;™ Soul Purpose™; True2Life; Vitalagy™; (DrinkACT) CLR Roasters; Cafe La Rica; Gigi Hill; RicoLife; Nature's Pearl; Renew Interests LLC; Mialisia; and others.

BeneYou, LLC. BeneYou was created in 2018 by combining M. Global, Jamberry and Avisae. Jamberry was purchased by M. Global after announcing it was closing[58] and then combined with Avisae to create the new company, adding former CEO of USANA Health Sciences Dave Wentz as their chairman.

Direct Sellers Acquired by Retailers

In the past, retail companies have purchased direct selling companies to gain access to a new channel of distribution, a company's products or to leverage the direct seller's cash flow. Here are a few examples with the stated purpose of the acquisition:

1973—Gillette acquired Jafra and grew the company from $8 million in sales to $250 million when it sold the company to a PE firm in 1998.

2005—Sara Lee exited the direct selling business by selling its portfolio of companies to Tupperware for $557 million. Sara Lee's businesses produced revenue of $470 million and included Avroy Shlain,

---

sale-of-beauticontrol-assets-to-youngevity-international-300571398.html, accessed June 24, 2019.
[58]   https://www.cbsnews.com/news/jamberry-nail-wraps-has-its-beauty-product-reps-in-a-jam-m-network-merger-fail/, accessed May 29, 2019.

House of Fuller, House of Sara Lee, NaturCare, Nutrimetics, Nuvo Cosmeticos and Swissgarde.[59] Sara Lee acquired Avroy Shlain as part of its purchase of Kiwi in 1994 and Lee acquired Fuller Brush (House of Fuller) in 1968.

2017—New Age Beverages Corporation (NASDAQ: NBEV) acquired Morinda Holdings, Inc for $85 million. The press release argued that the merger would create "the 40th largest non-alcoholic beverage company in the world with $300 million in net revenue, $20 million in adjusted EBITDA, $200 million in assets, no debt, and $40 million in cash and working capital." It also said that the "combination brings a leading portfolio of healthy beverages, with multi-channel penetration spanning traditional retail, e-commerce, and in-home; with a hybrid route-to-market spanning direct-store-delivery (DSD), wholesale, and direct-to-consumer."

2017—Coty Inc. (COTY.N) acquired Younique, LLC, buying a 60% stake in Younique for about $600 million.[60] Coty intends to allow Younique to operate without close supervision. According to the news release, "This partnership will combine Younique's high growth e-commerce platform and social selling direct-to-consumer business model with Coty's beauty product R&D and innovation know-how, as well as its extensive manufacturing and supply chain capabilities."[61]

---

[59]   https://www.businesswire.com/news/home/20050810005384/en/Sara-Lee-Corporation-Announces-Sale-Direct-Selling, accessed May 29, 2019.
[60]   https://www.reuters.com/article/us-coty-stake-younique-idUSKBN14U1Q6, accessed May 29, 2019.
[61]   http://www.cfo.com/ma/2017/01/coty-younique-beauty-products/,   accessed May 29, 2019.

Beyond Direct Selling

With the tremendous cash flows in direct selling and the challenge most companies have in deploying capital effectively for growth, historically a few direct sellers have attempted to use their cash to purchase non-direct selling businesses. Direct selling companies and/or their owners have been known to invest in other channels, though this happens more often outside the company than within the company. It is possible to acquire a direct selling company with the plan of using the cash to expand one's portfolio outside of the space. The examples found don't necessarily support such a strategy. Here are a few examples of capital deployed outside of direct selling by companies and/or their owners:

- **Avon owned Tiffany & Company from 1979-1984**
- **Forever Living owns a portfolio of Resorts (Forever Living Resorts) and ranches**
- **The Amway Grand Plaza Hotel is owned by the Amway company**

Direct selling owners who have invested in other businesses include:

- **Home Interior's Carter family owned the Dallas Mavericks (Purchased for $12 million)**
- **Amway owners purchased the Orlando Magic**
- **USANA founder Dr. Myron Wentz built Sanoviv Medical Institute, an alternative health hospital in Rosarito, Mexico—a fully licensed hospital and health resort.**

Liquidity Options

One of the most experienced direct selling investors is Eric Roth of MidOcean Partners. Eric spent 13 years as an advisor on the investment banking side of transactions before agreeing to join MidOcean with an emphasis (among other things) on the direct selling channel. When I interviewed Roth for this book, he said he believed there are potentially more liquidity venues in direct selling than the average consumer business. We'll examine of few of these liquidity options here.

Strategic Buyers

While the universe of strategic buyers in the traditional sense of a larger company acquiring a smaller company in the same industry is not as common or as attractive among direct sellers, there are a growing number of strategic buyers who tend to come from three categories:

- **Product Category Conglomerates**
- **Direct Selling Channel Conglomerates**
- **Larger Private Equity Funds**

Product category conglomerates are large, typically international and most often public companies that have a strategy of diversifying through acquisitions in their same product category. Their goal is often to acquire companies that are in multiple geographies, or have different demographics, or are competing in different channels of business. A few examples of the product category conglomerates that have made acquisitions of direct selling companies are:

Beauty and Personal Care

Coty Inc. (COTY.N) acquired Younique, LLC

Groupe Rocher acquired Arbonne

Beverage

New Age Beverages Corporation (NASDAQ: NBEV) acquired Morinda Holdings

Direct selling channel conglomerates are rarer and range from small privately held companies to large international direct sellers purchasing their first portfolio company. Most of the transactions of direct selling conglomerates to date are characterized as small and often without cash. There are, however, a few examples of direct sellers that can hardly be described as conglomerates but have purchased other companies and allowed them to remain independent. For example, German direct seller Vorwerk acquired and has operated Jafra Cosmetics as a stand-alone company. Revisit the discussion above on "Portfolio Strategies" to learn more about smaller portfolios being assembled in the channel.

Finally, there are the strategic buyers who are **larger private equity funds.** MidOcean partner Eric Roth cited TPG's investment in Rodan+Fields as one good example of larger private equity funds willing to be active in direct selling. Another example is The Raine Group's acquisition of Beachbody (a company whose primarily channel of distribution is direct selling). Though not announced publicly, Beachbody was apparently purchased from LNK by The Raine Group[62] and the transaction was confirmed in a conversation with Beachbody's CEO Carl Daikeler. LNK did announce its successful exit in a press release that included this detail:

LNK Partners is pleased to announce the successful exit of our minority investment in Beachbody. Beachbody is a leading creator and marketer of fitness and weight-loss solutions such as T25, P90X, INSANITY, 21 Day Fix, and Shakeology. During LNK's investment period, the company significantly expanded its direct selling business and successfully launched its online streaming service, Beachbody On Demand, which now has over 1.5 million subscribers and continues to grow rapidly.[63]

In the same release Daikeler said, "In 2012 when LNK invested in Beachbody, it quickly became clear we had chosen the perfect partner. The insights and assistance we got from the LNK team were so important, helping us navigate the fast-changing environment, grow our business rapidly and profitably, and do so while maintaining our unique company culture. Our relationship with LNK has been a real success story, and I'm proud to say six years later that we are a much stronger company, teed up for our next phase of growth."

David Landau, managing partner of LNK, added, "It has been a privilege for LNK to partner with Carl and the Beachbody team. This transaction not only represents an excellent result for our investors, but

---

[62] https://www.linkedin.com/in/rob-pietroforte-a5101013/, accessed May 29, 2019.
[63] https://www.pehub.com/2019/01/lnk-exits-beachbody/#, accessed June 15, 2019.

very importantly also positions Beachbody for continued success for many years to come."[64]

Public Offering

While the channel does have a few respected public companies, there has not been a public offering that I'm aware of since Mannatech went public in early 1999. I asked Douglas Lane of research house Lane Research, one of the world's foremost experts on public direct selling companies, if he believes there is an opportunity for more public direct sellers in the future.

"I would think so," he replied. "Private equity firms need exit strategies and there are good quality direct sellers that would be excellent in the public markets, like Stella & Dot or Rodan+Fields. There is no reason they shouldn't be public companies if that's the route that their investors choose to go. Down the road I would think there are candidates like Modere and doTERRA[65] and other companies that have private equity investments."

I asked Nu Skin CEO Ritch Wood the same question. He pointed out that the cyclical nature of direct selling makes it difficult for companies to meet the expectation of consistent and steady growth that most public equity investors expect to see. However, Wood believes the discipline of being public would bring value to many companies in the channel.

"Blake Rooney, who founded Nu Skin, said his philosophy was always that going public will be the best way to sustain a long-term business,"

---

[64] Ibid.
[65] I do not believe doTERRA has private equity investors.

Wood explained. "Going public, you're really forced to continue to innovate and drive growth or else the shareholders sort of get upset, and before you know it there's a new management team. Going public isn't the easiest route but it forces a discipline that oftentimes private companies don't have."

Debt Recapitalization

One of the reasons Eric Roth is so bullish on direct selling is because it both produces strong cash flows and has very little need to re-invest that capital to grow the business. In other words, the companies are producing truly free cash flow.

"If you own a direct selling business doing twenty-five to thirty percent EBITDA margin on two hundred million of revenue, you are spinning off fifty million in cash," Roth said. "There's not a lot of working capital required."

This combination of variables makes them excellent candidates for debt recapitalization. Roth acknowledged that a few companies were severally impacted because the debt was obtained at a peak EBITDA without consideration for a possible correction. When the correction came, the company was unable to repay the debt and shareholders lost their equity.

There are just as many examples of companies that have successfully recapitalized, and some on multiple occasions. Roth cited an example he is not at liberty to name when the private equity investor recapitalized a company four times in as many years and produced a 4x return on their investment without surrendering any equity. He explained the opportunity with this example:

"You've invested in the business at one hundred million and it was doing twenty million in EBITDA. Let's say you bought seventy percent of it for nine times—essentially a one hundred eighty million valuation. And let's say you put one hundred million in debt. So, on the eighty million of

equity someone rolled twenty-five to thirty percent and you wrote a fifty-five million equity check.

That twenty million in EBITDA grows to fifty million over six years because you are growing rapidly. Your average cash flow on that is probably thirty-five to forty million.

Over five years, you're definitely paying down that one hundred million note very quickly and re-leveraging it about two hundred million as a pure dividend.

So, your fifty-five million may have turned into one hundred-ten million in five years—meaning you could have returned two times your money, and you still own seventy percent of the business and be five years in.

The owners with thirty percent would be able to do the same thing. They might be able to take out three times on their thirty percent over a six-year period.

And if you're in my world, three times deals are big winners all day long. And so, when you go to exit, even if you exit it at seven times, you've made five times your money."

Direct selling companies should be impressive producers of free cash flow. These cash flows often become the primary interest of professional investors and time and time again private equity partners convince founders to cash out with a debt recapitalization. While this is an attractive option to investors, it has also been the villain of most of the colossal PE investment failures in the channel. If recapitalization is the central part of an investor's plan to ensure an ROI, there are two data points that should be considered:

"Debt Free Claims." On the soft side of the business, be aware that many (it was once "most") direct selling distributors make it a point to talk frequently about the fact that the company they represent is "debt free." Distributors used to make that claim while recruiting other distributors only as a casual reference to make the argument that the company was financially sound. With the near fatal or total collapse of several high-profile companies in the past decade, distributors are now more attuned to the risk of debt and for many career minded distributors, the debt free claim is an important consideration.

Plan for a Correction. Most of the deals that have led to bankruptcies or fire sales were those that made borrowing covenants based on the peak revenues the company had experienced. When the cycle of correction hit, the burden of debt forced management to make decisions and to react in ways that further destabilized the company and in many cases the correction turned into a free fall.

Cash Buyouts

Because of the excellent free cash produced by direct selling companies, the option to buy out investors with cash from operations and/or with cash from a large investor group is also an excellent option. There are examples of investors who earned their expected above average ROI and were able to exit with both parties happy. Unfortunately, because many of these deals were private, most people aren't aware of them.

Investors who approach direct selling with a plan to add and help create value should find that their investment can be very profitable. Those who see the channel as an opportunity to use financial wizardry to cash in on peak revenues with no thought for a potential correction will likely initiate a transaction that will leave their fund or their partners (debt providers, founders, and distributors) holding an empty bag.

We have talked about the investor's ability to create value through the use of capital or the use of capital transactions. In the next chapter we will talk more about the value investors can add to direct selling companies as advisors and business partners.

Chapter 11

Being a Great Board Member or Advisor

When asked what value investors could add to their direct selling business, one CEO I interviewed said, "Well, they'll be offended by this statement, but what they best bring is capital. This is a unique space and if they don't have experience in the industry then they should just let management do its job."

This CEO is not alone in that sentiment, but just two interviews into the nearly thirty I would complete, Asma Ishaq, the CEO of Modere, reminded me of the positive experience I had working with LNK Partners while a member of the Beachbody Board of Directors. Ishaq had a similar experience with Z Capital and her board of advisors at Modere.

"Many people have horror stories about working with a PE company or ownership that doesn't understand their business," she said. "To the contrary, I've actually had an absolutely amazing experience. Among several reasons as an example, I have weekly touch points with higher level reminders of our objectives ... they invest the time to understand our channel-specific critical performance indicators. I find this level of accountability and the firm's support to be incredibly valuable to and a competitive advantage of our company."

My interview with Ishaq inspired this chapter and convinced me that the objective of this guide should be to better inform, prepare and inspire not only investors but also board members, advisors, and partners who are new to direct selling.

When done right, direct selling companies can create enough value to enrich all members in the eco-system. Founders and investors can experience three- to five-X returns or more. Employees can have rich and rewarding careers. Distributors can earn and grow in ways they never imagined, and the customer can hire the perfect solution they need along with the support of a trusted advisor—all at a price they're happy to pay.

This virtuosity of value, however, is in a world where each participant has a long-term view of the business and where no one tries to extract "get rich quick" returns at the expense of others. Without the discipline of public markets or a long-term view, customer value can be sacrificed to pay distributors unsustainable rates of commission, owners can ignore the training and personal development needed to mature the field and investors can encourage a company to recapitalize with leverage that ignores the cyclical nature of the channel's revenues.

Board members and advisors can help companies make wise decisions and avoid the traps that leave one or more stakeholders damaged. After reading this guide, you should be able to identify those companies and practices that will drive maximum long-term value and be able to avoid being either the victim or cause of a company's failure.

While most professional investors will be familiar with how to structure financial deals, my experience is that these professionals are poor partners once they get around the board and begin advising their direct selling executives. The CEOs I interviewed for this book told me time and again that too often board members and capital partners failed to understand the nuances that make direct selling different than any other channel.

Direct selling companies need great board members and advisors and need more insight from smart people who bring experience from other industries. This chapter will help advisors learn how to prepare to be more valuable and will focus you on areas where you can make an impact.

Introducing Board Members to Direct Selling

Mauricio Domenzain was introduced to direct selling after a ten-year career in traditional retail as a partner in his family's import/export business. He said his first realization that this was an entirely new experience came as he observed the field's response to business mistakes.

"In retail, every transaction is business," Domenzain said. "If you miss a deadline or are out of stock on a product your customer wants, you pay a financial penalty and as long as it doesn't become a habit, both parties move on without a thought about it. In direct selling, every transaction is personal. If you fail to deliver on an order, there is someone you know on the other end and likely they have made a promise to a friend or family member that they now can't fulfill. Most people don't understand how personal this industry is and how central relationships are to success."

Domenzain served as a country manager in Mexico and then began to run more of a business in the United States and other Latin American countries. He loved what he was doing and decided he would let his brothers take the family company and he would invest his capital and life in building his own direct selling business. After a long and thorough search, he found Immunotec, a then public company trading in Canada. Domenzain completed the due diligence and negotiated the offer to take the company private. He then decided to select a private equity firm to join him in acquiring Immunotec. He and his partners began running Immunotec in December 2016 and completed the transaction in May 2017.

Having been a mid-career newcomer to direct selling, Domenzain realized that if his financial partners were going to be great business partners, he needed to provide them with adequate training and a thorough introduction to the channel. He invited his partners to participate in a board/advisor training program that I believe covered the key components of what every new advisor needs to know. Domenzain's new advisor training program included the following pieces:

Attending Events. Every new business partner was invited to attend a company event (ideally one field-led and one company-led). They didn't participate in the events but rather came as an unidentified attendee. Domenzain said these events gave the new partners the best introduction to the company and helped them understand the culture and the importance of gathering. Domenzain's partners have an open invitation to all events—especially the annual convention. He said they all attend and always feel like they gain value from the experience.

Formal Training. Domenzain prepared a full week of training (three to four hours per day) where he introduced them to every aspect of the business with an emphasis on the cost and value of events and incentives. He said that because events and incentives represent the largest "discretionary" spending for most companies, he felt it was important that his partners thoroughly understand the purpose and importance of them, so they viewed them as he did: as an *investment*, not an *expense*.

Compensation Plan Training. More than one CEO told me how important it was for new executives and advisors to receive thorough compensation plan training, but Domenzain added a twist that I think is brilliant: he invited one of his top leaders to come in and meet with the partners and do his best to sell them on the opportunity. Not only did Domenzain's partners receive great compensation plan training, but they also saw firsthand how the most effective field leader taught the plan and used it to recruit new distributors.

I remind you of a quote from the beginning of this book from Terrel Transtrum, who has introduced hundreds of successful business leaders to direct selling;

"I find that one hundred percent of what somebody knows about business outside of direct selling covers about seventy percent of what a direct selling company needs."

Make sure you insist on working with your direct selling portfolio company to get the training you need to close the knowledge gap. Following Mauricio Domenzain's simple three-point plan above is the best place to start.

Opportunities to Contribute

Outside advisors, financial partners and board members who take the time to become familiar with the companies they are working with can add tremendous value. When asked where CEOs can best utilize their help, here are a few areas of particular need:

Financial Discipline

When Dave Wentz resigned as the CEO of USANA Health Science, he had recently concluded tenure as chairman of the Direct Selling Association board and was then serving as the chair of the Direct Selling Education Foundation. For obvious reasons, his counsel and advice were highly sought-after commodities, and so he ended up visiting with several smaller direct selling companies. He came away from those consultations surprised how little discipline existed in many of the companies he advised.

"Planning is just seat-of-the-pants, go, go, go!" Wentz said. "And maybe that's just the entrepreneurial style in all industries. I've only seen direct selling, but it definitely feels like there's not enough business training and understanding and financial guidance and oversight to make sure that these things don't just shoot up and then disappear."

Investors can add great value to direct sellers by helping them put in place financial and management disciplines. Be prepared to help companies access, review, interpret and employ the learnings they can get from their own data. Help your companies impose planning discipline and improve communication. Author, speaker, and former direct selling financial executive Devin Thorpe has also had the chance to work with several direct selling companies and spoke with me about the value financial partners and outside board members can bring to companies.

"It's all value that the CEO and CFO are going to resist, maybe even hate," Thorpe said. "And it's incredibly important. They [financial partners and outside board members] have got to bring the discipline."

I asked Thorpe to elaborate on what he means by "discipline."

"If I were the lead investor," Thorpe replied, "I would say to the CEO and CFO 'Okay, let's schedule right now six or twelve board meetings each year. Let's know when they're going to be and let's understand the level of preparation required for an effective board meeting.

"CFO, you come prepared, and you deliver board books electronically seventy-two hours before the meeting. Your monthly numbers are delivered on the tenth of the month. And if you can't do that this week that's fine, we will help you figure that out so that within ninety days, you're closing the books no later than the tenth of the month.

"You will have robust reporting available for executives. You will have real-time reporting of all kinds of data that is transparently available to the private equity investors. Literally real-time dashboards with sales, commissions, enrollments and other data that's not being hidden or manipulated.

"That's the value a private equity investor brings," Thorpe concluded. "Imposing that kind of discipline on the company, and then specifically adding to their strategic preparation."

Relationships

It is no secret that one of the most valuable assets an investor can contribute is his/her personal network and relationships. Even the CEO I referenced in the opening paragraph of this chapter, when pushed, admitted that the "banking relationships and vendor relationships can add value." Many direct selling companies have not had experience accessing capital markets and have little experience nurturing banking relationships beyond their treasury needs. Many have a strong network that will help them find direct selling executives to fill open positions, but when it comes to finding operations, legal, finance or technology experience, most companies will find their network lacking, and will welcome the help of their board and advisors.

Improve the Management Team

In 2012, LNK Partners announced a minority investment in Beachbody and early in 2013 the company expanded its board to include LNK Partners. As an executive and then a board member, I had a front row seat to watch how a leading PE firm works with their new entity. I could write a book extolling the professionalism of the LNK team, but what was most valuable to Beachbody was our new partners' ability to bring world-class talent to augment our management team from day one.

LNK helped Beachbody find key talent and helped recruit them to the company. The LNK Partners introduced us to consultants who provided immediate value and helped expand and improve Beachbody's partner relationships in many key areas including technology, finance, and operations.

Adding new management or replacing current management is not the only way good advisors can help their portfolio companies. Most of the companies you invest in will lack systems and processes to evaluate and develop the management team they currently have. In a channel that is so vocal about personal development for its field sales representatives, it is shocking how little personal development is in place for the company's management and employees.

Best Practices

Because of the uniqueness of our channel, too often direct sellers have little if any experience bringing in advisors or consultants. Modere's CEO, who joined the channel after a long career elsewhere, observed that the channel tends to be more "insular" than others she has worked in. Some leaders struggle to reach out beyond their personal circle of friends to hire talent or gain experience. The result is that some companies are ignorant of many of today's best practices. Investors can help companies expand their knowledge and increase the management's team desire to improve.

Social Validation

Direct selling distributors are quite aware of society's lackluster perception of the channel. Despite the social coolness to their work, many distributors have had such a positive experience that they believe critics are simply ignorant. Still, most involved in the channel have an underlying desire for their work to be accepted by society. Direct sellers crave social validation.

To fill this need, companies seek validation wherever they can find it. Nu Skin became Olympic Sponsors during the 2002 Olympic Games in Salt Lake City. AdvoCare, Herbalife, and LifeVantage have their names on the jerseys of MLS soccer franchises. USANA has its name on a concert venue, and Amway on a stadium. Companies seek endorsements from athletes, invite ex-Presidents and public figures to speak at conventions, and engage in significant public giving campaigns all as part of their efforts to prove to the public—and themselves—that they are legitimate.

Social validation in direct selling is a critical component of a company's recruiting and retention efforts. Given how important this is for your portfolio company, as a new partner or board member you might ask what you can do to help. Here are three simple ways:

Express Confidence in the Company. When a deal is public, often a short on-stage statement from a managing partner explaining what the firm sees in the company will help. This type of effusive praise is not typically of value to companies in other channels, but it can be helpful in direct selling. Charles H. Esserman, president and CEO of TSG, may regret this statement in hindsight, but here is what he said when TSG invested in MonaVie:

"Since founding TSG, I have invested in many companies that I am very proud of, which have become enormous consumer brands," said Esserman. "With so many passionate and capable people working together, MonaVie has the potential to dwarf the growth of all of the brands we have participated in building. This is a once-in-a-lifetime opportunity for TSG, based upon the future outlook of MonaVie and its potential to help people on so many levels."

Make Introductions*:* Professional investors can help their direct selling companies by making introductions to noteworthy board members, medical advisory board participants or famous persons who can serve as public advocates.

Help Manage Risk: At the very least, professional investors can bring greater awareness to vulnerabilities and help the company address weakness to prevent (or create a plan to respond to) a potential crisis.

Chapter 12

How I Would Invest

We've covered a lot of ground in this book. I've given you an excellent foundation from which to make your investment decisions and provided you with my best learning, as well as thoughts from several of the channel's most experienced CEOs and consultants. What I haven't told you is what I would look for if I were investing in direct selling.

I Would Avoid

Before I summarize what I would do as an investor, let me make clear what I would *not* do. I would not invest in a company that:

Has yet to experience a correction. This channel has produced too many one hit wonders; companies that had a great run but could not convert that run into a sustainable business. Many companies have seen their sales soar then fall and stabilize. The great companies have seen three to five dips in sales but have figured out how to expand to new markets, reinvent their messaging or introduce new products— something to regain growth. If you can't resist a company in momentum, at the very

223

least please don't buy into a valuation that assumes continued growth. I made that plea to one private equity investor who assured me that their deal could produce a positive ROI even at sales 75% below the company's current sales, and he found out—the hard way—that I was right.

Is buying distributors or recruiting them from other companies. There may be a company that proves me wrong on this, but I have seen too many companies watch their massive growth turn to free-fall decline when the distributors they bought met resistance and decided to go find an easier opportunity. These MLM mercenaries remind me of the Iraqi soldiers that former Secretary of Defense Donald H. Rumsfeld described to reporters as troops who "just leave and melt into the countryside."[66]

Is focused on "opportunity" first. The days of recruiting distributors with an "opportunity" message are not entirely gone, but they are fading and will likely retire with the baby boomers.

I would also NOT undertake a merger and acquisition strategy unless it was clear that I was a holding company and the entities would remain independent. Although Blythe made a bad bet when it invested in Visalus, the company did an effective job selling itself as a holding company and keeping distributors from being concerned about the other direct selling companies it owned.

---

[66] https://www.cbsnews.com/news/iraqis-surrendering-in-hordes/, accessed May 30, 2019.

I Would Invest

Here are the most important attributes of a company I would invest in:

The Product/Service

Consumable Product. I would want a product that is consumable and/or a service that the customer will need over and over again.

Immediate Benefit. Direct selling companies that can demonstrate an immediate value or benefit to their product have always been easier to sell than products that require consumers to invest in a far-off return. The benefit could be a better value than they will find in other channels, but most of the time it's a product that has a "wow" impact on the user, like Younique's mascara, Beachbody's fitness programs or Herbalife's "lose weight now, ask me how" products.

Friends and Family Deal. Too few companies have figured this out, but my experience has taught me that a company will grow more quickly if its sales reps feel like they have something special to offer. In a world where relationships are becoming increasingly more important, companies need to learn how to honor friendships. Friends don't like to feel like a transaction is one-sided, like "you're making money on me." They don't mind their friends receiving a benefit IF they also receive something special in the deal. Friends and family expect an insider deal and direct selling won't shake its reputation until it resolves that core dissonance.

The distributor has a reason for being. Consumers are wary of middle men. They have been taught that they can get a better deal if they bypass them. Direct selling companies need to define a clear role for distributors that consumers see as adding value in a transaction.

The Company

Led or started by a founder with a purpose. Enduring direct selling companies are a crusade, not just a business opportunity. Founders with a vision that is broader than just making money tend to build sticky organizations and create companies that distributors want to sell for and customers want to buy from. While it would not be a requirement that a company is still led by the founder, I would be looking for a company founded with a broad vision that is easy to enroll others in accomplishing.

Organic Growth. When I interview management, I'm listening to hear them say, "We're not like other companies because this is the first time most of our distributors have ever done network marketing." I'll bet on first timers every time.

Product First. I'm looking for a company with a recruiting message that is product first; that has a culture that supports that message and product pricing that I consider a fair value.

Progressive Management. Direct selling companies need to evolve and most have a huge opportunity to improve their use of technology. Surprisingly, some companies are led by management that doesn't see the need to unite their high-touch model with a high-tech strategy. I would only invest in a management team committed to evolving.

Timing

In momentum. Everyone likes a company in momentum, but I would invest in momentum only if the deal allowed me the capital to survive a downturn and stabilization.

Before Momentum. I'd prefer to invest in a company that has nailed the model but not yet scaled. This is the preferred timing, but it's very difficult, especially when considering most PE's minimum capital requirements.

Post Momentum. The best and most likely opportunity to invest is with a company that has had steady and consistent growth (double digit but not triple digit) or a company that has hit its peak, declined and found a steady state (flat, or preferably high single-digit or low double-digit growth).

A Selling System

If I could not identify the sales system that was working for the field, or if I was uncertain about the system I would implement in a company, I wouldn't invest.

Conclusion

In Chapter 1, I quoted Zen Media's CEO Shama Hyder, who said that the direct selling company's "inherently social model has the potential to make them uniquely suited to a marketplace in which trust, relatability, and a strong network are critical features of a competitive edge."[67] She questioned the channel's ability to become socially-savvy enough to realize the opportunity to pivot and become mainstream. As direct selling insider, I believe some companies will pivot and many won't, but a select few—with the help of socially-savvy investors and advisors—will leverage all the benefits of direct selling to create extraordinarily valuable enterprises. I hope reading this book will help you identify those companies and will prepare you to be great partners with them in creating and realizing tremendous value.

I hope this book has helped you gain a deeper understanding of direct selling and increased your confidence and interest in investing. I would love to hear about your experience and continue to be an asset to your team as you invest in or advise direct selling companies. Please feel free to connect with me on LinkedIn (www.linkedin.com/in/brettblake) and I'll be happy to help you myself or introduce you to someone who can.

Finally, for many executives, direct selling is as much a mission as a job. This book would be incomplete if I didn't introduce you to the softer side of our channel and allow you to better understand why we believe the model has merit, virtue and is worth investing in and improving. I hope you'll take time to read the remarks I've included in the Epilogue from several of the CEOs I interviewed for this book. I believe you'll come away with a new appreciation for the value, fulfillment and opportunity that direct selling can provide to leadership, distributors, customers and investors alike.

---

[67]   https://www.forbes.com/sites/shamahyder/2017/08/14/why-direct-sales-companies-need-to-reach-the-end-consumer/#285750f612a4, accessed May 30, 2019.

Epilogue

At the end of the day, the direct selling company you are analyzing may not be a good fit for your financial portfolio, but many of us believe the channel is the best place to invest one's time and energy. We enjoy this channel, not because of the personal financial returns available (and there are plenty of examples of families and individuals who have built lasting wealth), but because of the opportunity this channel gives us to make a meaningful impact on individuals and families all around the world. As an epilogue to this book, I thought it important for potential investors and board members to learn the "why" behind the channel, so I've asked a few current and former executives to share their thoughts.

Ritch Wood, CEO, Nu Skin Enterprises

When asked if there was one thing he wished investors could understand about direct selling, Ritch Wood, CEO of one of the channel's largest public companies, Nu Skin Enterprises, replied:

I wish they could see the side of the business that you and I get a chance to see. The person who is busting their tail having nothing to make ends meet and they are able to start a business on the side using social selling, and it works great! They can now have a little money to put food on the table. I wish investors could understand what's behind the business rather than just the dollars and cents they are investing. I think when they see that side and really understand it, it changes their perspective. If you're just doing it for the short-term to make a buck and flip it, I think that's a risky proposition, and it's really not good. It's not good for all the people involved in that company.

The reason we want to be part of it is because at the end of the day, we are changing lives all around the world by giving people hope and opportunity they didn't have before. There are not that many businesses out there that actually have that touch to a person's life.

That's what I wish investors would be able to understand.

Craig A. Fleming, CEO/President, ServiceQuest Global Direct Sales Division

When I began my career in direct selling, I realized very quickly it was a vehicle that I could use and understand to get to where I wanted to be financially in life. I quickly discovered that while the money was important, it was just the tip of the iceberg behind the real power and passion that began to develop within me as I began helping others to succeed. My mentor told me, 'To be great in this business all one has to do is sell more than anyone else in the company, but if you want to be remembered in life—and for most people that is a very deep seated desire—you must become a builder of people.' It was at that moment that I discovered my "Why". I wanted to make a difference in people's lives by helping them to learn the skills they needed to be successful. Direct sales has given me that opportunity for over forty years and is still the most rewarding part of my professional consulting career.

Lori Bush, Chairwoman of the Board of Managers, New Avon, LLC

I came to direct selling because I believed it to be the best marketing channel for bringing innovation (in skincare) to market. Traditional Food/Drug/Mass (FDM) and Department Store distribution was cluttered and costly and therefore elicited a high degree of risk aversion, even for larger, more established brands. Direct-to-consumer channels oftentimes did not create the level of engagement needed and Direct TV was limited by availability or lack of access to airtime. The affiliations created by a direct selling program created a level of brand and product advocacy that would not otherwise be available to or accessible by challenger brands.

However, I stayed with direct selling because of the social impact. I am a true believer that the key to wellbeing and happiness is being part of something bigger than yourself. When done with integrity, the number of lives that can be positively touched through this business model is so meaningful. And the friendships that develop transcend the business and are priceless.

Bouncer Schiro, Chairman and CEO, Stream Energy

Bouncer stepped away from his operating role as CEO of Stream for several months and returned to his previous role with a renewed enthusiasm for the channel. In our interview, he said that during his time away he was surprised to find that he "fell in love with this industry again. It is the purest form of micro-entrepreneurship if it's done right."

Nancy Bogart, Founder and CEO, Jordan Essentials

Not only does direct selling enable millions of people to be micro-entrepreneurs, but many of the companies are founded by individuals who took a non-traditional path to business ownership. There are few who bought their way or advanced their way to ownership, and many more who started with an idea and ended up with a company. Nancy Bogart is one of those who accidentally found the path, but once on it was tenacious in making her company a success. She said:

Some people dream of starting a business. I was not one of them. I wanted to be a semi-stay at home mom and needed flexibility and an income. It only took one person to share with me what the Direct Selling Channel was and what it could do for my friends and family for me to say 'Yes!' I had been selling my bath and body line successfully on weekends. The power of people added to my product line helped me quickly understand the power of skipping the stores. I was hooked and within our first five years, we were named Missouri Chamber of Commerce Top Ten fastest growing business.

We have weathered the recession and many more ups and downs than I can count. The people we serve and the products we share have given me the strength to continue. I can look back and honestly say it was when I first fell in love with the people and the path in which we sell our products that has led to our nineteen-year success story. I am still in love after all of these years!

Travis Ogden, Chief Executive Officer, ISAGENIX INTERNATIONAL

Travis Ogden has made a big impact in the channel after leaving professional services to join a corporate team and has had the opportunity to serve three companies all with a very different approaches to growing their business. Despite the differences in his corporate experiences, ultimately, he has decided to remain in the channel because of the good he has seen among the customers and distributors he has served. He said:

Having started my career on a traditional professional services firm track, I eventually had the opportunity to experience this industry first hand and fell in love with it for three primary reasons: 1) the innovative products I see brought to market in this channel, 2) the opportunity it gives people to take control of their life on many levels, and 3) the personal development inherent in the channel. I consistently see everyday people join this industry and grow into better versions of themselves than they had ever dreamed possible. These stories motivate me to positively impact more lives with what we do.

Dave Wentz, former CEO of USANA Health Sciences and current Chairman, BeneYOU, LLC

Dave Wentz represents a group of leaders who are trying to understand how the Gig Economy and the power of mobile technology will impact the future. Dave took more than a year to learn from some of the world's most advanced thinkers and then came back into direct selling with a very bullish opinion of the future. He said:

I personally believe that direct selling will be the primary career opportunity of the future. Not necessarily the form of direct selling we have today, but an evolved model utilizing technology, data and the transfer of value within our connected community of humanity. Jobs are dying and entrepreneurship is the way to fulfill the purpose and passion that gives our lives meaning.

Jarom Webb, President, ASEA

Webb is one of the channel's up and coming executives with a similarly bright view of the future of direct selling. Webb came from public accounting and eventually was part of the founding team of what is now a global direct seller. He said:

Direct selling is a very powerful business model. Beyond the economic potential, direct selling allows you to connect with, understand, and respond to your customer base in a very deep and intimate way. It's about sharing one-on-one, face-to-face with trusted friends and colleagues. This direct connection and social selling environment create a compelling opportunity to bring unique and innovative products to the market, and it is where I believe the future of distribution is headed.

But what is most fulfilling for me personally about direct selling done with purpose, substance, and integrity is the life-changing impact that products, financial opportunity, and culture can have on so many people. It's about helping individuals and families create the life they want to live, giving purpose and rich meaning to their lives. I have experienced this with thousands of people all over the globe. That is what ultimately drives me.

Paul Adams, Adams Resource Group

Mary Kay Ash, the legendary founder of Mary Kay Cosmetics, was quoted as saying, "Ideas are a dime a dozen. People who implement them are priceless." Ideas aside, most of the leaders who have made direct selling their career describe a love affair with the people. Paul Adams has more than 30 years in the channel and now heads his own consulting firm, Adams Resource Group. Here is what he had to say about his love of the people in direct selling:

I suspect my entry into direct selling wasn't that much different than many others. It was an accident. I came from a completely different business world but once I stumbled into it, I found something really special—the people. When I started to get close to the folks that started and ran successful companies, I found a large group that truly wanted to help people achieve their dreams. Some dreams are large, some are small. They don't judge the dreams of others. They just try to provide a way for people to achieve them. They work to provide good products as well as good communities where doing good work and giving back is an expectation. They tackle the fundamentals of the business and focus on the people.

I've worked on the supplier/ partner side my entire career and I know that community is made of great people as well—working hard to help companies do good things.

Then, there are the people who are trying to change their lives—the dreamers—the field sales force. I've seen looks on their faces of incredible reward and satisfaction. I've seen determination. And I've seen their desires to help others as well. This is where the real wins are and the reason everyone is working so hard.

Products change and evolve. Comp plans come and go. There will always be a new "sexy" technology. I like all of the advancements and the opportunity to learn and grow with change. It keeps us young and on our toes. I like the unique business model and the challenges that come from it. But, in the end, good people will always be good people. I've been fortunate to be able to work with people I like and respect. They are my *friends. And, THEY are the reason I've been in this industry for over thirty years and will stay until they kick me out.*

Jeff Hill, Co-President, Team Beachbody (retired)

My former colleague Jeff Hill, who until recently was leading Beachbody's direct selling division, quickly set his skepticism aside and has learned to love the channel. He said:

Having entered this industry as somewhat hesitant and a skeptic, I soon discovered an undeniable power that coursed through the veins of this business model and especially in those companies whose authentic focus was products and people. It is a tangible spirit of hope and entrepreneurship. This is an industry whose fulcrum is not simply the sharing of believed in products, but more critically, that an individual must contribute to others in order to be successful. That formula further mandates continued personal development, learning, and elevation in order to lead and help others.

But wait, there's more. This industry democratizes opportunity for anyone willing to work, grow and contribute. Whenever an organization or industry can provide an opportunity to 'Live' better, 'Love' what you do and who you do it with, 'Learn' more, and finally have the potential to leave a lasting 'Legacy,' there is a stunning passion and power that flows from that business model. I have personally witnessed too many who have significantly changed their lives for the better through this unique channel to believe otherwise.

I also love this industry because there's an 'economics of goodness' that many companies emanate and when leveraged with integrity also proves extremely financially rewarding. Needless to say, I am no longer a skeptic nor hesitant about what this industry can offer.

Roger Morgan, CEO and Founder, pawTree

Direct selling companies aren't all founded by former distributors or moms with a desire to make a difference. Just west of Dallas, pawTree is building a community of direct sellers who are passionate about their pets. The founder, Roger Morgan, is as experienced a business mind as they come. He is a Harvard Business School graduate with a career that has included KPMG, the Boston Consulting Group (BCG) and time as president and CEO of a CPG pet products company called the Retail Products Group. With all of this experience, when it came time for Roger to launch his own company based on a commitment to premium pet products, he chose direct selling. He described it this way:

I did not set out to start a direct selling company. In fact, I had very little knowledge of the industry. When I founded pawTree I set out to launch an incredible line of premium pet nutrition products that would make a profound difference in the lives of pets and people. Having been in the pet industry a long time, I knew the importance and power of word of mouth advertising from one passionate pet person to another. We trust each other. As I considered the options for marketing and selling our products, I learned more about direct selling and felt confident this would be the best strategy for building a sustainable business. I had no idea how my heart would be changed forever. After five years in the industry, what brings me the most joy in building and growing this company is watching the lives of these women and men transform. I'm humbled and honored and grateful to have made so many new forever friends.

Brett Blake, Author

I had the good fortune of starting my career in direct selling, leaving to earn my MBA from Harvard Business School and then after a time in retail and software, returning to the channel. In other words, I found my way out and didn't have to return, but I chose to do so. I returned despite the fact that I had opportunities elsewhere, and despite the fact that I was well aware of the channel's not-so-positive public perception.

I returned to the channel and remain involved because of the people. As you have learned in this guide, I have not just recorded my own random thoughts in all of the previous pages, but rather a summary of the thoughts and ideas of nearly thirty other executives whom I shouldn't know. These executives are the leaders of companies many would call competitors. We compete on one level, but for the most part the executives in direct selling are friends in the truest meaning of the word. We pick up the phone when others call and do our best to answer questions, share our experience and provide support. Yes, the channel is full of amazing field leaders, but it is also led by high integrity executives who have become good friends to me and a great support to me in writing this book.

Thirty minutes east of Los Angeles lives a leader who reluctantly became involved in direct selling as a young woman. She was active in her church, lived the life of a busy mom, and worked part-time for just above $10 an hour taking calls to help pay the bills. The founder of a new direct selling company knew her and invited her to be a "ground floor" distributor in his company because he knew she was widely respected due to her high moral values. At first, she said no because she didn't want to "take advantage of friends." She was surprised to hear that this was the precise reason why the founder wanted her to be one of his distributors: he wanted to build a company that helped and didn't hurt friends and family.

This busy young mom—Traci Morrow—eventually agreed to join the company. I met her five years later when I was hired to lead that company. In only a few short years, Traci's income had grown to the average base salary of a private equity partner and her life had changed dramatically. She had adopted two children from Africa, had joined her husband to lead several missions there and was one of the largest contributors to her church. Her friendships had blossomed, and she found herself leading and mentoring women like her all across America. Success hadn't changed her, but she had used the earnings to magnify her influence on the world and to continue to make an impact.

Traci Morrow is one of thousands of distributors I've met who have made me proud of what I do. With the good comes the bad, of course—in biblical terms, there is some chaff in the wheat of our channel. But I know of no other vehicle that could take someone with a heart and a willing mind like Traci Morrow and give her the opportunity to earn the resources that allow her to be a great mom, an influence for good in her community and a life, health, and business coach to thousands around the world. As her website once stated, "For 20 years Traci Morrow has helped others live and write their own story. She will teach you how to prepare your life for success instead of repairing it!" Traci lives up to that promise and more.

I take great satisfaction in knowing that I helped ensure that Traci Morrow and others like her had the opportunity to fulfill their life's mission. After all, that truly is what direct selling is all about.

If you are interested in helping to scale social selling, as an advisor or investor, I would love to be a resource to you in your effort. Feel free to reach out to me via email at bblake@investingindirectselling.com.

Appendix: Deals and Resources

Most of the direct selling executives I've worked with throughout my career are of the opinion that there is very little if any M&A happening in the channel. When these executives read this appendix, they will be surprised by the number of deals that have taken place, and perhaps even more shocked to learn how many new companies are being launched at the time of this writing. For example, one of the consulting companies interviewed for this book claims to have launched more than 200 direct selling companies. They claim to be launching three to five new companies every month. With that much private activity happening, it would be difficult to publish an exhaustive list of the venture capital deals done in the channel, but I've tried to summarize many of the most notable ones here for your reference.

Capital Transactions

1946

Avon: *Initial Public Offering*[68]

1989: Mary Kay joined forces with other investors to form Chartwel

---

68   https://www.referenceforbusiness.com/businesses/A-F/Avon-Products-

Associates, and purchased a 19.8 percent share of Avon.[69]

1990: Avon Sells 40% stake in Avon Japan in Japan IPO for $218 million.

1968

Mary Kay, Inc.: *IPO*

1985: Company goes private in a deal valued at $315 million and $336 million.

1989: Mary Kay tried to take over Avon Products, but was unsuccessful.

1991: Chartwell sold most of its shares, leaving Mary Kay with a three percent share of Avon.[70]

Fuller Brush Company: *Acquired by Consolidated Foods, now Sara Lee Corporation.*

1991: The company was placed in private ownership.

1994: It became a subsidiary of CPAC Inc.

2007: Acquired by Buckingham Capital Partners.

2012: Acquired by David Sabin and Victory Park Capital.

2018: Acquired by Galaxy Brush LLC[71]

1982

Primerica: *IPO on OTC Board.*

Inc.html, accessed May 30, 2019.

[69]   http://www.fundinguniverse.com/company-histories/mary-kay-inc-history/, accessed May 30, 2019.

[70]   http://www.fundinguniverse.com/company-histories/mary-kay-inc-history/, accessed May 30, 2019.

[71] https://en.wikipedia.org/wiki/Fuller_Brush_Company, accessed May 30, 2019.

1983: Lists on NASDAQ as ALWC (AL Williams).

1987: Acquires brokerage firm Smith Barney for $750 million.

1988: ALWC acquired MILICO from Primerica Corporation through a stock merger, making Primerica Corporation the majority shareholder of ALWC. Sanford Weill's Commercial Credit acquired Primerica Corporation for $1.54 billion, retaining the Primerica name.

1989: Primerica Corporation began trading on the New York Stock Exchange.

1993: Primerica acquired the remaining 73% of Travelers Insurance Corporation and adopted the name Travelers Inc., which was changed to Travelers Group.

1998: Travelers Group and banking giant Citicorp merged creating Citigroup.

2009: Citi announced spin-off Primerica through an initial public offering.

2010: Citi raises $320 million in IPO and stock opens at $15 and closes at $19.65 a share. Warburg Pincus acquires 23 percent stake in Primerica, with warrants for another 10%.

2011: Primerica purchases ~nine million shares from Citigroup for ~$200 million. Citigroup sold its remaining eight million shares a month later to complete the separation.

2013: Warburg Pincus LLC sells 2.5 million shares of Primerica Inc., cutting its stake to 4.4 percent[72]. Primerica buys out Warburg Pincus for $154.7 million.

---

[72]   https://www.law360.com/articles/414723/selldown-brings-warburg-pincus-close-to-primerica-exit, accessed May 30, 2019.

1986

Herbalife: *Initial Public Offering*

1993: Secondary offering of five million shares for $28 million in proceeds.[73]

2002: Acquired for US$685 million by J.H. Whitney & Company and Golden Gate Capital, which took the company private again. 2004: IPO on the NYSE of 14,500,000 common shares at $14 per share, netting the owners $1.3 billion.

1989

Shaklee Corporation: *Yamanouchi Pharmaceutical acquires Shaklee for $395 million.*[74]

2004: Acquired by Activated Holdings for $310-Million.[75]

1993

Amway: *Amway Corp. made an initial public offering of the subsidiary, Amway Asia Pacific Ltd., in an effort to finance the company's entry into China. The offering of 7.9 million common shares was priced at $18 each and was quoted at $29 by day's end.*[76]

---

[73]   https://www.bloomberg.com/news/articles/1993-09-12/a-wonder-offer-from-herbalife, accessed May 30, 2019.

[74]   http://www.fundinguniverse.com/company-histories/shaklee-corporation-history/, accessed May 30, 2019.

[75]   https://www.dmnews.com/channel-marketing/direct-mail/news/13078367/shaklee-acquired-in-310m-deal, accessed May 30, 2019.

[76]   https://www.apnews.com/a56c8f46423ad3f75ee78008fe0045ba,   accessed

2000: Amway completed buybacks of shares of Amway Asia Pacific Ltd. AAP, and Amway Japan, Ltd., it's only publicly-held subsidiaries.[77]

1995

Rexair: *Acquired by Jacuzzi Brands (a.k.a. US Industries).*
2005: Rhône Capital acquires 70% stake in Rexair.
2014: Jarden Corp acquires Rexair from Rhone Capital[78] *(Jarden acquired by Newell Rubbermaid).*
2019: Newell Brands agreed to sell Rexair business to Rhône Capital. No financial terms were disclosed.[79]

1998

Jafra Cosmetics: *Clayton, Dubilier & Rice, Inc. (CD&R) purchased from Gillette (purchased by Gillette in 1973) for $200 million and invested another $77 million of equity.*
2011: CD&R takes out $154 million in a $275 million recapitalization.
2012: CD&R sold its 84% interest in Jafra Cosmetics to Vorwerk & Co. KG for a reported 5x return.

May 30, 2019.
[77] https://www.marketwatch.com/story/amway-corp-to-reorganize, accessed May 30, 2019.
[78] https://mergr.com/jarden-acquires-rexair, accessed May 30, 2019.
[79] https://www.pehub.com/2019/02/rhone-to-buy-rexair-business-from-newell-brands/, accessed May 30, 2019.

Home Interiors & Gifts: *Hicks, Muse, Tate & Furst Inc. paid $920 million for control of Home Interiors. In 1997 the company had nearly $469 million in sales and a profit of $62.2 million.*

2006: Highland Capital Management LP takes control after acquiring Home Interiors' debt.

2008: Home Interiors files for bankruptcy and sells all but Home Interiors' Mexican and Canadian subsidiaries as well as Domistyle, Inc. to Penny and Steve Carlile, who fold it into Celebrating Home.

Nu Skin: *Acquires retail nutritional supplement company Pharmanex for estimated $105.5 million in stock, debt, and cash.*

1999

Oriflame (German): Industri Kapital bought 45% of Oriflame's shares while the company was listed on the London Stock Exchange. With this transaction, Oriflame was delisted from the stock exchange. Industri Kapital valued Oriflame at approximately 450 million Euros.

2004: Management listed the company on the Stockholm Stock Exchange through an IPO and Industri Kapital started selling its shares on the stock exchange and exited August 2006.[80]

---

[80] https://www.worldofdirectselling.com/private-equity-direct-selling/, accessed May 30, 2019.

2000

BeautiControl, Inc.: *Acquired by Tupperware Brands Corp. for $60 million.*[81]

2017: Tupperware Brands Corporation (NYSE: TUP) sold Beauticontrol assets to Youngevity International, Inc. (NASDAQ: YGYI)[82]

Creative Memories, Inc. (Antioch): *Acquired in $200 million debt deal by ESOP.*

2008: Files for bankruptcy protection.

2013: Files for bankruptcy a second time

2014: Emerges from second bankruptcy with an acquisition by Caleb Hayhoe, Chairman of Flowerdale Group Ltd.

Nature's Sunshine Products: *Acquired Synergy WorldWide Inc. for approximately $4.7 million in cash.*[83]

2003

Pampered Chef: *Warren Buffet's Berkshire Hathaway bought Pampered Chef a few days after Buffett reviewed its financials. By 2001, the company's annual sales reached $740 million.*[84]

---

[81] https://callcenterinfo.tmcnet.com/news/2008/05/02/3422115.htm, accessed May 30, 2019.

[82] https://www.prnewswire.com/news-releases/tupperware-brands-announces-sale-of-beauticontrol-assets-to-youngevity-international-300571398.html, accessed June 15, 2019.

[83] https://www.naturalproductsinsider.com/archive/natures-sunshine-acquires-worldwide-financial-holdings-0, accessed May 30, 2019.

[84] https://www.worldofdirectselling.com/private-equity-direct-selling/, accessed

2004

Arbonne: *Harvest Partners purchased NPG, Arbonne's parent company. Arbonne filed for bankruptcy in 2009. The company restructured the debt to equity and the company's lenders became the owners. The company officially declared bankruptcy in January 2010. But in several weeks, Arbonne emerged from bankruptcy.*
2008: Groupe Rocher announced it entered into a definitive agreement to acquire Arbonne International.

LR Health & Beauty Systems (German based): *Apax Partners invested in LR and then gradually acquired a majority share.*
2012: Apax Partners agreed to sell its stake to a private equity consortium of Bregal Capital and Quadriga Capital.

2006

5LINX: *Trillium Group and the New York State Common Retirement Fund made a $1.7 million investment in 5LINX.*
2014, New York State Comptroller's Office reported this investment had generated a $6.7 million return—close to four times the original investment.[85]

May 30, 2019.

[85] https://www.worldofdirectselling.com/private-equity-direct-selling/, accessed May 30, 2019.

Modere (a.k.a. Neways International): *Acquired by Golden Gate Capital*

2012: Z Capital Partners, L.L.C. and funds affiliated with S.A.C. Capital Advisors, L.P. become owners as part of the restructuring. Golden Gate Capital maintains an equity stake.

2013: Z Capital Partners buys out S.A.C. Capital Advisors

Stream Energy: *Raised $10 million growth capital from NGP Energy Capital Management.*[86]

2007

Ambit Energy: The *former Chairman and CEO of Home Interiors & Gifts Inc., Donald J. "Joey" Carter, Jr., joins as an investor and advisor.*[87]
Date Unknown: Hunt Consolidated Investments acquired a <23% interest.

2008

MonaVie: *TSG Consumer Partners made a significant investment in MonaVie, for a small, minority equity interest in the company.*

2015: Jeunesse Global (Jeunesse), a leading direct selling company devoted to inspiring healthy living and youth enhancement, announced the acquisition of MonaVie. The company was reportedly sold for less than $20 million.

---

[86] https://mystream.com/company/press/2006-2-24-retail-energy-provider-stream-energy-raises-10m-n-growth-capital, accessed May 30, 2019.
[87] https://www.ambitenergy.com/about-ambit-energy/press-releases/joey-carter-joins-ambit-energy-investors, accessed May 30, 2019.

Visalus: *Blyth, Inc. (NYSE: BTH) closed on the second phase of its acquisition of ViSalus Sciences and owned 57.5% of the company. Blyth made its initial investment in ViSalus in August 2008.*[88] *2014: ViSalus co-founders, along with "certain shareholders," agreed to reacquire 70.9 percent of ViSalus, raising their stake to 90 percent.*

Worth Collection: *L Catterton made an equity investment (amount not disclosed).*[89]
2016: New Water Capital, L.P. (New Water) acquired The Worth Collection, Ltd.[90]

2010

Stella & Dot: *Sequoia Capital invested $37 million in Stella & Dot, valuing Stella & Dot $370 million. The company had previously raised about $5 million from Radar Partners.*

Silpada Designs, Inc.: *Avon Products, Inc. (NYSE: AVP) agreed to purchase all of the assets of Silpada Designs, Inc. for $650 million.*

---

[88] https://www.streetinsider.com/Corporate+News/Blyth%2C+Inc.+%28BTH%29+Closes+57.5%25+Acquisition+of+ViSalus+Sciences/6431607.html, accessed May 30, 2019.
[89] https://www.linkedin.com/in/davedefeo/, accessed May 30, 2019.
[90] https://www.newwatercap.com/new-water-capital-acquires-worth-womens-apparel/, accessed May 30, 2019.

2013: Company founders repurchase the company for $98 million.
2016: Assets purchased by the Richline Group Inc., a wholly-owned subsidiary of Berkshire Hathaway.

Avon Japan: TPG Inc. agreed to buy 75% stake in Avon Japan for 7.3 billion yen ($89.7 million) and made a tender offer for the rest of the publicly traded unit.
2016: Acquired by Keystone Partners.
2018- South Korea's LG Household & Health Care purchase for 10.5 billion yen ($96.3 million)

Isagenix: Cyprium Partners invested to refinance existing debt.
2011: Cyprium made an additional equity investment to provide partial liquidity to certain shareholders.[91] I'm told through a source who asked not to be named that this equity was repurchased using cash from operations.
2018: Sold 30% of the company to The Isagenix Employee Stock Ownership Trust[92]—a debt deal estimated at $375 million. Also acquired $40 million revolving credit facility.[93]

[91] http://www.cyprium.com/investment-portfolio/prior-investments/, accessed May 30, 2019.
[92] https://maadvisor.com/MANY/2018-MANY/17th_Annual_MA_Advisor_Awards_Winners_List.pdf, accessed May 30, 2019.
[93] https://www.moodys.com/research/Moodys-assigns-B2-CFR-to-Isagenix-outlook-stable--PR_382111, accessed May 30, 2019.

2011

LegalShield: *Acquired by MidOcean Partners through a cash transaction valued at approximately $650 million.*[94]
2018: Stone Point Capital LLC ("Stone Point") entered into a definitive agreement to acquire a majority interest in LegalShield.[95]

Youngevity International, Inc.: *Javalution Coffee Company, which was trading under ticker symbol JCOF, completes reverse merger into Youngevity Essential Life Sciences resulting company became Youngevity International, Inc. in July 2013.*
2019: Completes $3.6 million public offering Series B Convertible Preferred Stock.

Gigi Hill: *Maveron invests $3 million for minority interest.*[96]
2018: Sold to Youngevity International, Inc. (NASDAQ: YGYI)[97]

2012

Beachbody: *LNK Partners announced that it made a minority investment in Beachbody, LLC. The size of LNK's investment and other terms were not disclosed.*

---

[94] https://www.worldofdirectselling.com/private-equity-direct-selling/, accessed May 30, 2019.
[95] https://www.businesswire.com/news/home/20180227006144/en/Stone-Point-Capital-Acquire-Majority-Stake-LegalShield, accessed May 30, 2019.
[96] https://www.directsellingnews.com/maveron-invests-in-gigi-hill/, accessed May 30, 2019.
[97] https://www.directsellingnews.com/youngevity-acquires-gigi-hill-brand/, accessed May 30, 2019.

2019: LNK Partners sold their interest in Beachbody to The Raine Group.

Cabi: *"Cabi" stands for "Carol Anderson by Invitation" was bought from its founders by the private equity firms Irving Place Capital and J.H. Whitney. Cabi's revenue then exceeded $250 million.*
2017: Sentinel Capital Partners acquired Cabi Holdings Co LLC.

GeneWize Life Sciences, Inc.: *Capsalus Corp. (OTCBB: WELL) acquired GeneWize Life Sciences, Inc., the wholly-owned direct-selling subsidiary of GeneLink Biosciences, Inc. (OTCBB: GNLK).[98]*

Matilda Jane Clothing: *Received $9.5 million from CID Capital.[99]*
2017: Webster Capital purchased Matilda Jane from CID Capital.[100]

2013

Hy Cite Enterprises, LLC: *Completed a recapitalization with Palladium Equity Partners. The terms of the investment were not disclosed.*

---

[98]   https://www.directsellingnews.com/capsalus-corp-completes-purchase-of-genewize-life-sciences-inc/, accessed May 30, 2019.
[99]   https://insurancenewsnet.com/oarticle/Private-equity-investor-seekign-150-million-%5BIndianapolis-Business-Journal-IN-a-406572#.XKvG2utKgXo, accessed May 30, 2019.
[100] https://pitchbook.com/newsletter/webster-buys-matilda-jane-in-sbo, accessed May 30, 2019.

Stella & Dot: *Sequoia Capital invested $37 million for a ten percent stake[101]*

Natura: *Acquires high-end retailor Aesop.*

2014

Jewel Kade: *Thirty-One Gifts announced the acquisition of Utah-based direct seller Jewel Kade.*

Origami Owl*: Gauge Capital made a reported $43 million investment in Origami Owl, a party-plan seller of fashion jewelry.[102]*

BeautyCounter: *TPG invested an estimated $10-$15 million in Series B (earlier round funded by TomorrowVentures).[103]*

2018: TPG and Mouse Partners invested $65 million at a reported $400 million valuation.[104]

Jamberry Nails: *Acquired by Wasserstein with co-investment of $3.4 million from Private Equity Holdings A.G.[105]*

---

[101] https://www.directsellingnews.com/stella-dot-receives-37-million-investment-from-sequoia-capital/, accessed June 15, 2019.

[102] https://www.bizjournals.com/dallas/blog/morning_call/2014/10/gauge-capital-closes-250m-fund-invests-43m-in.html, accessed May 30, 2019.

[103] http://campfire-capital.com/beauty/tpg-takes-stake-beautycounter/, accessed May 30, 2019.

[104] https://www.bloomberg.com/news/articles/2018-01-04/beautycounter-is-said-to-raise-about-65-million-in-new-funding, accessed May 30, 2019.

[105] www.piplc.com/system/files/rrp/reports/annual-report-2015.pdf, accessed May 30, 2019.

2018: Sold to M. Global.[106]

2015

Ruby Ribbon: *Raised $7.5 million in a Series C. The financing was co-led by DBL Partners and Direct Selling Capital. Previous investors Trinity Ventures and Mohr Davidow Ventures also participated in the round. Ruby Ribbon, which sells shapewear and women's clothing online, previously raised $11.8 million.[107]*

Blyth: *The Carlyle Group announced it would acquire Blyth for $98 million. Blyth was the parent company of PartyLite and the majority owner of ViSalus between 2012-2014. The price paid for shares represented a premium of approximately 105% percent over the closing price of Blyth common stock at that date.[108]*
2016: Carlyle merged PartyLite with Candle-Lite to form Luminex [109]

Pippa & Jean: *This jewelry social selling company closed on a 4M EUR investment by Seaya Ventures. Seaya joined previous investors Holtzbrinck Ventures, Vorwerk Ventures, ProSieben Sat 1 and Klingel.[110]*

---

[106] https://www.directsellingnews.com/m-global-jamberry-avisae-merge-into-beneyou/, accessed May 30, 2019.

[107] http://www.dblpartners.vc/2015/11/ruby-ribbon-raises-7-5-mln/, accessed May 30, 2019.

[108] https://www.carlyle.com/media-room/news-release-archive/carlyle-group-announces-agreement-acquire-blyth-inc-98-million, accessed May 30, 2019.

[109] https://www.carlyle.com/media-room/news-release-archive/carlyle-group-and-centre-lane-partners-combine-candle-lite-company, accessed May 30, 2019.

[110] seayaventures.com, accessed May 30, 2019.

Gold Canyon: *(Date is estimated) Acquired by Unique Investment Corporation.*

2016

Avon: Avon Products, Inc. ("Avon") and Cerberus Capital Management, L.P. ("Cerberus") close strategic partnership transaction separating Avon's North America (New Avon, LLC) business into a privately-held company majority-owned and managed by an affiliate of Cerberus. Cerberus invested $435 million in Avon in exchange for Avon convertible perpetual preferred stock. Cerberus has invested $170 million for an approximate 80% ownership interest. Avon maintains an approximate 20% interest in New Avon LLC. [111]

2019: LG Household & Health Care, Ltd. Acquired New Avon from Cerberus Capital Management and Avon Products for reportedly $120 million. [112]

Passion Parties Inc.: *Acquired by Pure Romance (competitor).* [113]

Pure Haven Essentials: *Acquired by Global Ventures Partners.* [114]

[111] https://www.prnewswire.com/news-releases/avon-products-inc-and-cerberus-capital-management-announce-close-of-strategic-partnership-transaction-300228820.html, accessed May 30, 2019.
[112] https://www.prnewswire.com/news-releases/lg-household--health-care-to-acquire-new-avon-llc-300838103.html, accessed May 30, 2019.
[113] https://www.cincinnati.com/story/money/2016/01/11/pure-romance-buys-intimacy-product-seller-passion-parties/78653006/, accessed May 30, 2019.
[114] https://www.providencejournal.com/news/20160802/ava-anderson-under-new-owners, accessed May 30, 2019.

Lulu Avenue: *Charles & Colvard, Ltd. (NASDAQ: CTHR), sold Lulu Avenue assets to Yanbal USA, Inc. for $500,000.*[115]

2017

Immunotec: Acquired by Immuno Holding, a company led by Mauricio Domenzain, and Nexxus Capital in a deal valued at $25 million.[116]

Jusuru International: Acquired by *Modere (formerly Neways), a portfolio company of Z Capital.*[117]

Younique LLC: *Coty Inc (COTY.N) bought a 60% stake for about $600 million*[118]

Natura: *Acquired brick-and-mortar retailer The Body Shop.*

Verve: *Raised $18.5 million in Series B led by VC Draper Esprit, and previous investors Kindred, Frontline Ventures and Backed.*

2019: Reported to be subscribed at $50 million in Series C (as of publication).

[115] https://www.charlesandcolvard.com/press/charles-colvard-announces-sale-of-main-lulu-avenue-assets-to-yanbal-usa-inc, accessed May 30, 2019.

[116] https://www.directsellingnews.com/immunotec-acquired-by-immuno-holding/, accessed May 30, 2019.

[117] https://www.pehub.com/2017/01/z-capital-backed-modere-to-buy-jusuru/, accessed May 30, 2019.

[118] https://www.reuters.com/article/us-coty-stake-younique-idUSKBN14U1Q6, accessed May 30, 2019.

2018

BeneYou, LLC: *M.Global, Jamberry and Avisae join together to form the newly launched BeneYOU, LLC.*

Rodan+Fields: *Announced that TPG Capital, the global private equity platform of alternative asset firm TPG, has made a strategic minority investment in the company.*[119]

2019

NATURA-AVON PRODUCTS: *Companies announced a merger that would leave Natura holding 76% of the combined business with over $10 billion in annual revenue. The deal is a stock agreement where Avon accepts 0.3 Natura shares for each Avon share. That values Avon's equity at around $2 billion, representing a 28% premium over its closing share price on May 21.*[120]

---

[119] https://www.rodanandfields.com/pages/press-leading-skincare-brand-rodan-and-fields-partners-with-tpg, accessed May 30, 2019.

[120] https://www.reuters.com/article/us-avon-prdcts-m-a-natura-cosmetic/natura-agrees-to-buy-avon-creating-cosmetics-powerhouse-idUSKCN1SS0G4, accessed June 15, 2019.

China Entry Deals

A few companies have used financial transactions for international expansion. Here are a couple of the deals I'm aware of:

Nature's Sunshine Products

2014: Nature's Sunshine Products, Inc. (NASDAQ: NATR), and Shanghai Fosun Pharmaceutical (Group) Co., Ltd. ("Fosun Pharma"; stock code: 600196-SH 2196.HK), a leading healthcare company in the People's Republic of China ("China"), announced a definitive agreement to form a China joint venture to market and distribute Nature's Sunshine and Synergy products in China and an investment by Fosun Pharma of approximately $46.3 million in Nature's Sunshine common stock to be issued pursuant to a private placement transaction. Nature's Sunshine intends to use the net proceeds of the private placement transaction to fund its share of the China joint venture and pay a special one-time cash dividend of $1.50 per share contingent upon transaction closing.[121]

USANA Health Sciences

2010: USANA Health Sciences, Inc. (NASDAQ: USNA) announced it acquired BabyCare Ltd, a China-based direct selling company to ultimately establish a business via BabyCare in China.[122]

---

[121] https://www.globenewswire.com/news-release/2014/06/26/646916/10087258/en/Nature-s-Sunshine-Announces-Strategic-Alliance-With-Fosun-Pharma.html, accessed May 30, 2019.

[122] https://www.businesswire.com/news/home/20100816006649/en/USANA-Health-Sciences-Acquires-BabyCare-Direct-Selling, accessed May 30, 2019.

Roll-Ups

The following companies have pursued a roll-up strategy and here I have listed all the deals I'm able to document:

Ariix: *Positions itself as a company "with multiple independent brands" allowing distributors "the ability to diversify your business. Each brand was designed to stand on its own and to work together." The company has announced the following acquisitions:*

> *2011: Trivani*
> *2018: NuCerity*
> *2018: ENVY Jewellery*

BeneYOU: *The company claims to be "a uniting of common values and purpose." It was founded in 2018 "with the coming together of M.Global, Jamberry, and Avisae.*

JRJR Networks: *Declared bankruptcy and its website was not operating as of the spring of 2019. Previously the company was known as "CVSL, earlier Computer Vision Systems Laboratories," and defined itself as "a holding company of multi-level marketing companies. JRJR Networks traded on the NYSE MKT." Acquired companies:*

> *2013: Longaberger Co.[123]*
> *2013: Your Inspiration at Home*

---

[123]   https://www.bizjournals.com/columbus/morning_call/2013/01/longaberger-acquired-by-docking.html, accessed May 30, 2019.

2013: Tomboy Tools

2013: Agel Enterprises

2013: Golden Girls[124]

2013: Paperly

2013: My Secret Kitchen

2014: Uppercase Living

2015: Kleeneze Ltd.

2015: Betterware, Ltd

Regal Ware: *Does not consider itself a conglomerate but rather a U.S. manufacturer that makes the "finest cookware for families," but it has made a few acquisitions in the cookware space. Acquired companies:*

1979: Saladmaster

1984: Kitchen Fair[125]

2018: ESPRO, Inc. (coffee & tea accessories)

Sharing Services Global Corporation (OTCQB: SHRG)

(formerly Sharing Services, Inc. (OTC: SHRV)): *Calls itself a "diversified holding company headquartered in Plano, Texas, that owns, operates or controls an interest in a variety of companies specializing in the direct selling industry."[126] Acquired companies:*

2017: Four Oceans Holdings, Inc. (travel)

---

[124] https://www.dispatch.com/article/20131011/BLOGS/310119712, accessed May 30, 2019.

[125] https://www.regalware.com/our-company/history/, accessed May 30, 2019.

[126] https://www.qualitystocks.com/sharing-services-inc-shrv-is-revolutionizing-the-direct-sale-industry/, accessed May 30, 2019.

2017: Total Travel Media, Inc.

2017: Medical Smart Care, LLC ("MSC")[127]

2017: 212 Technologies, LLC (marketing/direct selling software)[128]

2018: Direct Cellars Wine Club

2018: Legacy Direct (home entertainment)

Vorwerk & Co. KG: *Vorwerk is a privately held German company that has been owned by the same family for more than 130 years. The company has started or acquired a portfolio of direct selling companies and added them to stand alone brands launched by the company (Kobold and Thermomix). As of the end-2016, Vorwerk has subsidiaries in 22 countries, and trading partners or distributors in 56 others. 63% of the group sales is generated outside Germany.[129] Acquired companies:*

> *2001: Lux Asia Pacific (Thailand, Indonesia, Taiwan, Japan, the Philippines and Singapore)*

> *2004: JAFRA Cosmetics (USA and Mexico)*

Vorwerk Ventures: *In addition to its acquisition of operating entities, Vorwerk has a venture capital division that has invested in several direct-to-consumer companies. The company's website claims*

---

[127] https://www.equities.com/news/sharing-services-inc-shrv-invests-into-medical-smart-care-llc-for-additional-incentive-programs, accessed May 30, 2019.

[128] https://www.centralcharts.com/en/26721-sharing-services-inc/news/754624-sharing-services-inc-acquires-intellectual-property-rightsthrough-investment-in-212-technologies-llc, accessed May 30, 2019.

[129] https://www.worldofdirectselling.com/direct-selling-power-vorwerk/, accessed May 30, 2019.

that they "invest growth capital of between € 1 and 10 million in the form of minority interests in companies with an existing market presence. Our investment focus is on direct-to-customer business models." Vorwerk Ventures listed the following companies in their portfolio:

Current Portfolio (2019)

Dinner for Dogs

Stowa

Madchen Flohmarket

Junique

Horizn Studios

Vaniday

CrossEngage

Flaschenpost.de

Ottonova

Thermondo

Lillydoo

Smartfrog

Previous Portfolio

PAUL direkt

Ringana

DaWanda

ENJO

Neato robotics

Stylefruits.de

Tennis Point

Gestigon

MeinAuto.de

Hello Fresh

Pippa Jean

Zlesara

Youngevity (YGYI): *According to a leading consultant who claims to be familiar with Youngevity's strategy, "American Longevity (Joel Wallace and his son Steve) acquired Youngevity and assumed the name. Then they set on a course to acquire fledgling and flailing MLM companies, stripping off overhead and making them instantly profitable."*

The company currently describes itself as a "hybrid of the direct selling business model that combines the power of e-commerce with social selling. Under one corporate entity, YGYI has established a virtual main street of products that include top-selling retail categories like health/nutrition, food/beverage (including coffee), spa/beauty, home/family, apparel/jewelry, and other innovative services. Our products and services are distributed through a global network of preferred customers and distributors."

Here is a list of the acquisitions we have been able to document:

2004: Bio-lumin Essense (supplements)[130]

2011: JavaFit

2011: Ovation

2011: FDI[131]

---

130   https://www.nutraceuticalsworld.com/issues/2004-10/view_industry-news/american-longevity-acquires-mlm-start-up, accessed May 30, 2019.

131   http://beyondtangytangerine.net/2012/09/my-personal-experience-with-

2011: Javalution Coffee Company

2011: R-Garden (nutrition)

2011: Bellamora (skincare)[132]

2011: Adaptogenix International (nutrition)[133]

2012: Livinity, Inc. (nutritional products)

2012: GLIE, LLC dba True2Life (supplements)

2013: GOFoods Global[134]

2014: Good Herbs Inc (herbal supplements)[135]

2014: Heritage Makers (digital products)

2014: Restart Your Life (dietary supplements)[136]

2014: Beyond Organics, LLC (organic food and beverages)

2014: Biometrics International, Inc. (liquid supplements)

2015: PAWS Group, LLC (pet treats)

2015: Mialisia & Co., LLC (jewelry)

2015: JD Premium LLC (supplements)

2015: Sta-Natural, LLC (supplements)

2015: HempFx

2016: Sozo Global[137]

---

youngevity/, accessed May 30, 2019.

[132] http://ezinearticles.com/?An-Unbiased-Third-Party-Review-Of-Youngevity---Is-Youngevity-The-Real-Deal-Or-Just-More-Hype?&id=6414195, accessed May 30, 2019.

[133] http://mlminfosite.com/mlm-news-youngevity%C2%AE-acquires-adaptogenix-international/, accessed May 30, 2019.

[134] https://www.preparedfoods.com/articles/113174-youngevity-to-acquire-gofoods, accessed May 30, 2019.

[135] http://www.sddt.com/Health/article.cfm?SourceCode=20140505tqb&_t=Young evity+acquires+Good+Herbs#.XKvXGetKgXo, accessed May 30, 2019.

[136] https://www.businesswire.com/news/home/20141002005209/en/Youngevity-YGYI-Announces-Acquisition-Restart-Life, accessed May 30, 2019.

2016: Nature's Pearl[138]

2016: Legacy for Life[139]

2016: South Hill Designs (jewelry)

2017: Sorvana International (nutrition - includes FreeLife & L'dara)[140]

2017: RicoLife (tea)[141]

2017: Beauticontrol

2017: Bellavita (Mediterranean diet)

2018: ViaViente (Nutrition)[142]

2018: Gigi Hill (Handbag and Accessories)[143]

2019: Khrysos Global (CBD Manufacturer)

---

[137] https://www.businessforhome.org/2016/08/youngevity-acquires-renew-interests-llc-sozo-global/, accessed May 30, 2019.

[138] https://www.businessforhome.org/2016/08/youngevity-acquires-natures-pearl/, accessed May 30, 2019.

[139] https://www.businessforhome.org/2016/08/youngevity-acquires-legacy-for-life/, accessed May 30, 2019.

[140] https://www.marketwatch.com/press-release/youngevity-acquires-freelife-ldara-through-acquisition-of-sorvana-international-2017-06-19, accessed May 30, 2019.

[141] http://www.marketwired.com/press-release/youngevity-acquires-ricolife-otcqx-ygyi-2205429.htm, accessed May 30, 2019.

[142]   https://www.globenewswire.com/news-release/2018/03/06/1415790/0/en/YOUNGEVITY-INTERNATIONAL-COMPLETES-ACQUISITION-of-VIAVIENTE.html, accessed May 30, 2019.

[143]   https://www.globenewswire.com/news-release/2018/01/24/1304309/0/en/Youngevity-Acquires-Gigi-Hill-Brand.html, accessed June 15, 2019.

Conclusion

As you can see from the length of this appendix, there have been plenty of deals completed in direct selling. My hope is that there will be many more in the years to come, and that they will be better deals with higher average returns for investors like you who have read this guide and who have effectively selected and partnered with their portfolio companies.

Connecting With the Author

In addition to writing, Brett can be available for executive and board coaching/strategy sessions and speaking engagements. Brett also offers a free consultation for those with questions about the content of this book or about a transaction under consideration.

Brett can be contacted via email at:
bblake@investingindirectselling.com

"If you've found this book useful, please consider leaving a short review on Amazon."

www.ingramcontent.com/pod-product-compliance
Lightning Source LLC
Chambersburg PA
CBHW021514210326
41599CB00012B/1250